# Negotiating the
# Korea-Singapore FTA

The **Institute of Southeast Asian Studies (ISEAS)** was established as an autonomous organization in 1968. It is a regional centre dedicated to the study of socio-political, security and economic trends and developments in Southeast Asia and its wider geostrategic and economic environment.

The Institute's research programmes are the Regional Economic Studies (RES, including ASEAN and APEC), Regional Strategic and Political Studies (RSPS), and Regional Social and Cultural Studies (RSCS).

**ISEAS Publications**, an established academic press, has issued almost 2,000 books and journals. It is the largest scholarly publisher of research about Southeast Asia from within the region. ISEAS Publications works with many other academic and trade publishers and distributors to disseminate important research and analyses from and about Southeast Asia to the rest of the world.

# Negotiating the Korea-Singapore FTA

## A CASE STUDY

K. KESAVAPANY AND RAHUL SEN

ISEAS

INSTITUTE OF SOUTHEAST ASIAN STUDIES
SINGAPORE

First published in Singapore in 2007 by
Institute of Southeast Asian Studies
30 Heng Mui Keng Terrace
Pasir Panjang
Singapore 119614

*E-mail:* publish@iseas.edu.sg
*Website:* http://bookshop.iseas.edu.sg

*The responsibility for facts and opinions in this publication rests exclusively with the authors and their interpretations do not necessarily reflect the views or the policy of the publisher or its supporters.*

---

**ISEAS Library Cataloguing-in-Publication Data**

---

Kesavapany K.
    Negotiating the Korea-Singapore FTA : a case study / K. Kesavapany and Rahul Sen.
    1.   Free trade—Singapore—Case studies.
    2.   Free trade—Korea (South)—Case studies.
    3.   Korea (South)—Foreign economic relations—Singapore.
    4.   Singapore—Foreign economic relations—Korea (South)
    5.   Korea (South)—Commerce—Singapore.
    6.   Singapore—Foreign economic relations—Korea (South)
    I.   Sen, Rahul, 1965–
    II.  Title
HF1595 Z4K7K42               2007

ISBN 978-981-230-458-2 (hard cover)
ISBN 978-981-230-494-0 (PDF)

---

Typeset by International Typesetters Pte Ltd
Printed in Singapore by Utopia Press Pte Ltd

# CONTENTS

# FOREWORD

Singapore's total trade with the world is three times its gross domestic product, the highest in the world. It is not an exaggeration to say that trade has been, since 1819, the life blood of Singapore. The genius of Sir Stamford Raffles was to understand, nearly 200 years ago, that free trade will bring prosperity and that all peoples and nations benefit when trade and investment flow freely across borders.

At the APEC Leaders Meeting, in New Zealand, in 1999, APEC endorsed the legitimacy of using bilateral free trade agreements as a means to achieve multilateral trade liberalization. Following that historic decision, Singapore concluded its first free trade agreement with New Zealand. Since then, Singapore has concluded free trade agreements with many of its major trading partners, including the US, Japan, India, Australia and Korea.

We should encourage our negotiators and our scholars to write about our negotiations in order to document the unique features of each negotiation and to seek to learn lessons from them. I am, therefore, very pleased that two of my friends, Ambassador K. Kesavapany and Dr Rahul Sen, have co-written a case study of the Korea-Singapore Free Trade Agreement.

*Tommy Koh*
*Chairman, Institute of Policy Studies*
*Chief Negotiator, US-Singapore Free Trade Agreement*
*15 March 2007*

# PREFACE

Free Trade Agreements (FTAs) are viewed as superhighways that connect major economies and new markets. It is in the above context that Singapore has been engaged in negotiating bilateral Free Trade Agreements (FTAs) with its major trading partners who are "like minded" in terms of willingness to undertake comprehensive measures to liberalize trade and investment among themselves. Korea and Singapore, sharing the above vision on a variety of regional and international issues and having enjoyed strong political relations decided to embark on negotiations for a bilateral FTA in 2003. The conclusion of substantive negotiations of the Korea-Singapore Free Trade Agreement (KSFTA) was announced on 29 November 2004.

On 2 March 2006 Singapore's bilateral FTA with the Republic of Korea came into force. The Korea-Singapore FTA (KSFTA) is Korea's first comprehensive FTA involving any ASEAN member country and provides a framework for building a strong strategic and economic partnership between Korea and the ASEAN countries. It is therefore designed to be a building block in the process of community building efforts towards an East Asian Community in the long run.

The KSFTA is a comprehensive and highly substantive agreement, which is WTO-consistent in principles and WTO-plus in commitments. It aims to further enhance trade and investment flows between the two countries, bringing about a broadening and deepening of bilateral economic ties. The agreement covers diverse areas ranging from trade in goods, services and investments to that of competition policy, intellectual property protection, government procurement and other broad areas of economic cooperation. The book outlines the salient features of the agreement and the concrete benefits that would accrue to Singapore businesses and consumers from its use, in a range of areas beyond tariff reduction in trade in goods.

This book analyses and documents the rationale behind the KSFTA, and its impact on the economies of Korea and Singapore, underpinning the growing economic linkages between the two countries that have become stronger since the enforcement of the KSFTA. It studies how the progress of the FTA is being monitored and its implementation facilitated by Singapore government agencies. The aim of the book is to provide a better understanding of Singapore's FTAs and ways in which an FTA can be a building block for global free trade.

My colleague, Dr Rahul Sen, Fellow, ISEAS helped in the preparation of the draft manuscript and comments and offered suggestions at various stages of the writing of the book. I would like to thank the contribution of several senior diplomats, officials and scholars for their support and encouragement in writing this book. I would particularly like to thank Ambassador Tommy Koh for kindly agreeing to write the foreword and his words of encouragement therein. I would also like to thank officials from IE Singapore, Mr Tai Chew Thian and Mr Jad Ng, for agreeing to be interviewed on the subject.

I hope this book will be useful for negotiators, scholars, diplomats, businessmen, students and civil society from not just Singapore and Korea, but also from other countries, in helping them to have a better understanding of how FTAs provide a foundation for a strong economic and strategic relationship and facilitate stronger regional economic cooperation.

*K. Kesavapany*
*Director*
*Institute of Southeast Asian Studies, Singapore*
*6 June 2007*

# 1

# BACKGROUND TO THE KOREA-SINGAPORE FTA

## INTRODUCTION

Singapore has always been a leading advocate of global trade liberalization and is often placed in the league of "super-trading" nations. Its total trade volume is currently three times its GDP. Its growth strategy over the past decades has maintained a policy of outward orientation and reduced barriers to international trade and investment. Fully committed to the WTO, Singapore believes that it is the only mechanism that can ensure a fair, inclusive and predictable environment for all economies to engage in and benefit from trade. However, limited progress in the WTO on the multilateral trade and investment liberalization process in recent years has pursuaded it to simultaneously pursue the second and third tracks to trade liberalization through the regional and bilateral routes, in order to sustain its global competitiveness in the international market.

The move towards bilateral trade liberalization through the pursual of Free Trade Agreements (FTAs) was particularly evident in the aftermath of the East Asian crisis of 1997–98, and its resultant adverse impact on trade and liberalization efforts within ASEAN and the APEC. With the slowing down in the pace of and willingness of Singapore's ASEAN neighbours to undertake trade and investment liberalization, Singapore was persuaded to explore the third route of trade liberalization through bilateralism to advance freer trade in Southeast Asia. This strategy has been aimed at complementing its strong advocacy of multilateral liberalization. Singapore's policymakers are convinced that suitably designed regional and bilateral Free Trade Agreements can complement the WTO and help stimulate further global trade liberalization and play a catalytic role in moving the WTO forward.

Regional economic integration through these agreements has thus been recognized as a key element for increased competitiveness and long-term viability. The trends for bilateral and regional economic partnerships have been more pronounced in the last decade. These economic partnerships, while being diverse in nature, modality and coverage, all have one purpose in mind — to further liberalize the trading regime so as to reap the benefits of free and open trade. In this context, Liang (2005, pp. 13–14) notes:

> Singapore's pursuit of FTAs/RTAs has been driven by perceived economic benefits of regional integration as by strategic and political considerations. Singapore believes that FTAs complement the multilateral trading system in several ways:
> Firstly, FTAs can provide impetus to multilateral trade liberalization. FTAs allow countries to identify compatible partners with whom to pursue faster and broader liberalization, thus acting as catalyst for multilateral trade liberalization. Second, FTAs create positive competitive dynamics that spur further liberalization. FTAs put pressure on those that are slow to liberalize and in the process; help to push everyone towards liberalization at the regional and multilateral level. Third, FTAs engender the internal economic reform processes. FTAs can help governments to overcome domestic resistance to reforms of sensitive sectors. Governments may be more willing to initiate difficult domestic reforms if they can be carried out on a preferential basis and in measured steps. Fourth, FTAs improve the economic competitiveness of businesses and provide greater access to the markets of FTA partners...What is central is the need to ensure that FTAs/RTAs are WTO-consistent and WTO-plus whereby FTAs would contribute towards catalyzing the WTO liberalization process and regional integration... Beyond advancing Singapore's economic interests, Singapore believes that these intra and inter regional FTAs help to build a web of strategic linkages for Singapore within the region and with countries outside the region. They serve the broader strategic interest of anchoring the presence of its major trading partners in Southeast Asia, and ensuring that they remain stakeholders in Singapore and the region. The FTAs also help to sustain an open regional orientation that prevents the formation of inward-looking trading blocs. This web of interlocking economic and strategic interests will contribute to regional stability, security and prosperity.

FTAs are therefore viewed as superhighways that connect Singapore to major economies and new markets. It is in the above context that Singapore has been engaged in negotiating bilateral Free Trade Agreements with its major trading partners who are "like minded" in terms of willingness to undertake comprehensive measures to liberalize trade and investment among themselves. This strategy has also been interpreted as a way for Singapore to solve the "convoy problem" whereby least willing members within ASEAN could slow the pace of trade liberalization.

As of March 2007, Singapore has entered into bilateral FTAs with the US, Japan, Australia, New Zealand, the Hashemite Kingdom of Jordan, EFTA, India, Korea, Chile and Panama. It is also currently in the process of or contemplating negotiations with Mexico, Canada, Pakistan, Peru, China, and the Gulf Cooperation Council, among others.[1] It concluded a bilateral FTA with the Republic of Korea that came into force on 2 March 2006.

## THE LAUNCH OF THE KOREA-SINGAPORE FTA (KSFTA)

The KSFTA is Korea's first FTA involving any Asian member country, and is therefore significant. The idea of a Korea-Singapore bilateral FTA (KSFTA) was first raised in November 2000. The first public announcement of the FTA was on 6 November, when the Korean Trade Minister Hwang Doo-Yun made an announcement during an interview on Korean cable TV that Singapore was a "candidate for FTA negotiations after Chile" and that "it was difficult to conclude an FTA with 10 nations of ASEAN altogether due to their different conditions. First, we will map out an FTA with Singapore."

Korea and Singapore had agreed to launch a Joint Study Group at the meeting of the Trade Ministers of the two countries, which was held on 14 November 2002, on the occasion of the WTO Ministerial Conference in Sydney. The JSG, comprising representatives from government, business and academia, held three meetings from March to September 2003 to examine the feasibility and desirability of establishing an FTA between the two countries. The JSG also discussed the scope of the proposed KSFTA as well as key issues to be dealt with in the future FTA negotiations. The Joint Study Group (JSG) on the Korea-Singapore Free Trade Agreement completed its work and submitted its report to the Heads of State of the Republic of Korea and the Republic of Singapore, on 7 October 2003.

The report recommended that the scope of the KSFTA should include: a) comprehensive liberalization and facilitation of economic relations between

Korea and Singapore, which would include trade in goods and services, investment, government procurement, and intellectual property rights; b) a comprehensive range of economic cooperation elements covering an array of areas including financial services, information and communication technology, human resources development, trade and investment promotion and broadcasting; and c) consultation and dispute settlement mechanisms on issues arising from the interpretation and application of the KSFTA.

In view of these findings, the JSG recommended that both countries enter into formal FTA negotiations at an early date, using the JSG report as a framework, and aim at concluding the KSFTA negotiations and signing the relevant agreements within a reasonably short period of time. The conclusion of substantive negotiations of the Korea-Singapore Free Trade Agreement was announced on 29 November 2004.

The remainder of this monograph is organized as follows. The next chapter focuses on Singapore's trade and investment relations with the Republic of Korea. Chapter 3 analyses the implications of the Korea-Singapore Free Trade Agreement for bilateral economic relations. Chapter 4 focuses on the salient features of the KSFTA, and its expected benefits for Singapore. Chapter 5 analyses the post-KSFTA scenario with respect to its implementation. The final chapter concludes this monograph.

# 2

# SINGAPORE AND KOREA
## Expanding Economic Linkages

## INTRODUCTION

Historically, Korea and Singapore have enjoyed strong political relations, with both countries sharing the same strategic outlook on a variety of regional and international issues. The leaders of both countries have regularly held bilateral meetings at the margins of international fora, such as the World Trade Organisation (WTO) and the Asia Pacific Economic Cooperation (APEC) to exchange views on regional developments. Both countries have recognized the view that economic integration in the region is vital for enhanced competitiveness. In the above context, this chapter focuses on the current state of economic relations between Singapore and Korea, focusing on merchandise trade, trade in services and on investment flows between the two countries,[2] in order to emphasize the economic rationale behind the KSFTA.

## MERCHANDISE TRADE

Korea and Singapore have enjoyed strong economic linkages that have been driven by strong complementarities between both economies. In 2006, with total trade amounting to S$30 billion (about US$11 billion), Korea was Singapore's 9th largest trading partner (Tables 2.1 and 2.2), while Singapore was Korea's largest trading partner among the ASEAN countries, and overall the 10th largest trading partner of Korea. Over the 1993–2003, the volume of Singapore-Korea merchandise trade more than doubled at a compound rate of 9.5 per cent per annum. However, this growth was even more rapid at a compound annual average rate of 16.7 per cent over 2003–06.

**TABLE 2.1**

**Merchandise Trade between Korea and Singapore**

(In S$ million)

|  | 1993 | 1998 | 1999 | 2000 | 2001 | 2002 | 2003 | 2004 | 2005 | 2006 |
|---|---|---|---|---|---|---|---|---|---|---|
| Total Trade | 7,754 | 9,379 | 13,091 | 16,788 | 15,234 | 17,007 | 19,188 | 24,332 | 27,735 | 30,513 |
| Singapore's Domestic exports to Korea | 1,957 (59.0) | 2,020 (47.0) | 2,934 (49.0) | 4,279 (50.5) | 3,977 (47.4) | 3,812 (40.9) | 4,339 (41.1) | 4,911 (39.3) | 5,435 (40.5) | 5,591 (40.3) |
| Singapore's Total Exports to Korea | 3,326 | 4,292 | 6,028 | 8,479 | 8,391 | 9,316 | 10,551 | 12,481 | 13,412 | 13,876 |
| Singapore's Imports from Korea | 4,428 | 5,087 | 7,063 | 8,309 | 6,843 | 7,691 | 8,637 | 11,851 | 14,322 | 16,636 |

*Note*: Figures in parentheses indicate share of Singapore's Domestic Exports in its Total Exports.

*Source*: IE Singapore (2007).

Since Singapore is a regional entrepot, it is important to distinguish between what is directly exported from Singapore (Domestic Exports) and what is transhipped through Singapore to be exported to Korea from other ASEAN economies (Re-Exports). It is observed from Table 2.1 that the share of domestic exports in Singapore's total exports to Korea has actually declined over the 1993–2006 period from 59 to 40 per cent, indicating that re-exports have gained greater importance in driving Singapore's exports to Korea. Overall, Korea was Singapore's 7th largest export destination and 9th largest import source in 2006 (Table 2.3).

**TABLE 2.2**
**Singapore's Top 10 Trading Partners, 2006**
(In S$ billions)

| | | |
|---|---|---|
| 1 | Malaysia | 105.8 |
| 2 | United States | 90.3 |
| 3 | China, PR | 85.2 |
| 4 | Indonesia | 62.9 |
| 5 | Japan | 52.3 |
| 6 | Hong Kong, China | 49.8 |
| 7 | Taiwan | 39.3 |
| 8 | Thailand | 31.8 |
| **9** | **Korea** | **30.5** |
| 10 | Australia | 22.1 |

*Source*: IE Singapore (2007).

**TABLE 2.3**
**Singapore's External Trade for 2006**
(In S$ billions)

| Exports (Domestic and Re-Exports) | | | Imports | | |
|---|---|---|---|---|---|
| 1 | Malaysia | 56.3 | 1 | Malaysia | 49.5 |
| 2 | United States | 42.8 | 2 | United States | 47.5 |
| 3 | China, PR | 42.0 | 3 | China, PR | 43.2 |
| 4 | Indonesia | 39.5 | 4 | Japan | 31.6 |
| 5 | Japan | 20.7 | 5 | Taiwan | 24.2 |
| 6 | Thailand | 18.0 | 6 | Indonesia | 23.4 |
| 7 | Australia | 16.2 | **7** | **Korea** | **16.6** |
| 8 | Taiwan | 15.1 | 8 | Saudi Arabia | 14.7 |
| **9** | **Korea** | **13.9** | 9 | Thailand | 13.8 |
| 10 | India | 12.2 | 10 | Germany | 10.8 |

*Source*: IE (2007).

**TABLE 2.4**
**Composition of Merchandise Trade between Korea and Singapore in 2002**
(In US$ millions)

| | Korea's Exports to Singapore | | | Singapore's Exports to Korea | |
|---|---|---|---|---|---|
| 1 | integrated circuits semiconductors | 1,427 | 1 | integrated circuits semiconductors | 1,364 |
| 2 | wireless telecommunication equipment | 437 | 2 | peripheral storage units | 236 |
| 3 | ships | 335 | 3 | computers | 147 |
| 4 | gas oils | 332 | 4 | computer parts | 106 |
| 5 | petroleum | 102 | 5 | petroleum | 86 |

*Source*: Korea Customs Service (2003).

Table 2.4 shows the composition of merchandise exports between Korea and Singapore in 2002. It is observed that electronic products, viz. integrated circuits and semiconductors, telecommunication and ICT equipment and refined petroleum products, constituted the bulk of Singapore-Korea trade (Joint Study Group, 2003). This composition is believed to have been unchanged in recent years.

## TRADE IN COMMERCIAL SERVICES

In the current era of rapid globalization, various activities in the services sector, which were hitherto labeled as being non-tradable, are now being increasingly opened up for commercial trading purposes among international service providers. This has increased the need to specifically focus on trade in commercial services and gains from its liberalization not only at the regional level, but also at the bilateral level, with the KSFTA negotiations being no exception.

According to the WTO rankings of commercial services trade in 2005, Korea ranked 18th in global exports of commercial services and 12th in global imports of commercial services, accounting for 1.8 per cent of world service exports and 2.5 per cent of world service imports, respectively. In the same year, Singapore ranked 16th in the global export and import of commercial services, accounting for about 1.9 per cent of world service exports and imports, respectively (Table 2.5). However,

## TABLE 2.5
### Leading Exporters and Importers in World Trade in Commercial Services, 2005

| Rank | Exporters | Value (US $ billion) | Share (% of world total) | Rank | Importers | Value (US $ billion) | Share (% of world total) |
|---|---|---|---|---|---|---|---|
| 1 | United States | 354.0 | 14.7 | 1 | United States | 281.2 | 12.0 |
| 2 | United Kingdom | 188.7 | 7.8 | 2 | Germany | 201.4 | 8.6 |
| 3 | Germany | 148.5 | 6.2 | 3 | United Kingdom | 154.1 | 6.6 |
| 4 | France | 115.0 | 4.8 | 4 | Japan | 132.6 | 5.6 |
| 5 | Japan | 107.9 | 4.5 | 5 | France | 104.9 | 4.5 |
| 9 | China | 73.9 | 3.1 | 7 | China | 83.2 | 3.5 |
| 10 | Hong Kong, China | 62.2 | 2.6 | 12 | **Korea** | **57.7** | **2.5** |
| 11 | India | 56.1 | 2.3 | 13 | India | 52.2 | 2.2 |
| 16 | **Singapore** | **45.1** | **1.9** | 16 | **Singapore** | **44.0** | **1.9** |
| 18 | **Korea** | **43.9** | **1.8** | 20 | Hong Kong, China | 32.4 | 1.4 |
| | | | | 29 | Malaysia | 21.6 | 0.9 |
| | World | 2,415.0 | 100.0 | | World | 2,345.0 | 100.0 |

*Source:* WTO (2006).

both Korea and Singapore ranked among the top five service exporters and importers in Asia, indicating the significance of the services trade in their economies.

There is no known source of data on bilateral service trade in Singapore. However, Singapore aims to strengthen and consolidate its position as a regional and global services hub, specifically in the area of trade logistics, financial services, media, entertainment and education services. In this context, its current linkages with Korea's service providers assume importance. The KSFTA agreement, which focuses at length on services trade liberalization, is thus likely to generate major economic opportunities for both countries in the expansion of their bilateral services trade links.

## BILATERAL INVESTMENT RELATIONS

In 2002, Korea's investments in Singapore totalled US$41.2 million, while its total cumulative investment in Singapore amounted to US$862.0 million as of the end of that year. In comparison, the volume of investments flowing from Singapore to Korea has been much larger in magnitude, and cumulatively amounted to US$2.5 billion during the same period.[3] As of March 2007, Korea's total cumulative investments in Singapore amounted to nearly US$1.5 billion (Export-Import Bank of Korea, 2007).

Singapore was the 8th largest foreign investor (2nd largest among ASEAN countries after Malaysia) in Korea in 2002, with 48 cases of new investments worth a total of US$146 million. As of the end of 2001, the total cumulative investment was US$2.3 billion and this amount increased to US$2.5 billion as of the end of 2002. This was an increase of 6.2 per cent despite a 19.4 per cent drop in Korea's total FDI for 2002 (Korea-Singapore FTA Joint Study Group 2003).

With continued market liberalization and corporate reforms in Korea, Singaporean companies have grown their volume of investments in Korea, especially in the ICT services and infrastructure sectors. With a view to attracting investment from Korean companies, Singapore's Economic Development Board (EDB) has been working closely with the Korea's Small & Medium Business Administration (SMBA)[4] as well as the Korean private sector to help promote the Korea Venture Acceleration Centre (KVAC),[5] which was officially opened in Singapore on 21 March 2002. The Singapore Business Federation (SBF) and the Korean International Trade Association (KITA) also initiated in November 2003 a Korea-

Singapore Business Roundtable to increase interaction and cooperation between the private sectors of the two countries.

Singapore investments in Korea are mainly in sectors such as financial and real estate, with opportunities in lifestyle (spa services), food services and manufacturing and electronic and precision engineering (automotive and consumer electronics). Over the past few years, several prominent Singapore companies such as PSA International, Ascendas, City Development Limited, and Ya Kun Kaya Toast have established their presence in Korea.

In 2005, the estimated value for Korean Investments in Singapore was US$134 million, while Singapore investments in Korea amounted to US$389 million, indicating a growing and sizeable business interest on the part of companies from both sides. According to the Korea Ministry of Commerce, Industry and Energy, Singapore investments in Korea reached US$557 million in 2006, representing a significant increase of 43 per cent over 2005. Concomitantly, Korean investments in Singapore also increased to US$602 million, more than four fold expansion in just one year, during which the KSFTA was implemented (Figure 2.1).

**FIGURE 2.1**

**Trends in Bilateral Investment Flows between Singapore and Korea, 2000–06**

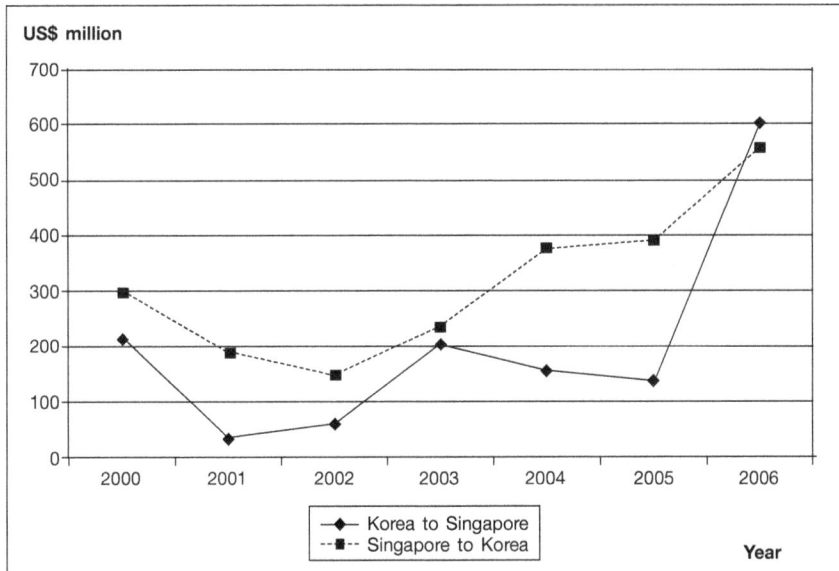

*Source*: The Export-Import Bank of Korea (2007).

The investment linkages between Singapore and Korea are predicted to grow further with the liberalization of investment norms under the KSFTA agreement. The agreement, which has focused to a large extent on liberalization of investment rules as well as on protection of intellectual property rights, is likely to provide a strong impetus for knowledge-based investments to flow between the two countries.

The above indicates that although economic linkages between Singapore and Korea appear well-established, there is much scope for further expansion of trade and investment flows between the two countries. The KSFTA is expected to play a facilitating role in this regard, by also helping to upgrade Singapore's and Korea's capabilities and competitiveness by exploiting their synergies for mutual benefit.

# 3

# KOREA-SINGAPORE ECONOMIC RELATIONS AFTER FTA
## Towards a Mature Partnership

## INTRODUCTION

This chapter[6] explores the implications of the Korea-Singapore Free Trade Agreement (KSFTA) for Korea-Singapore economic relations. It is organized as follows. Section 2 analyses Korea's Trade Policy Strategy and highlights the importance of FTAs. Section 3 analyses the current state of bilateral economic relations between the two countries. Section 4 analyses the implications of the KSFTA for bilateral relations, and concludes the chapter by providing strategies for win-win cooperation.

In 2005, Korea ranked 11th among the world's largest economies with a gross domestic product (GDP) of about US$790 billion. It was only the twelfth country to pass the US$500-billion mark in trade volume after countries such as the U.S., Germany, Japan and China. Between 1970–2004, Korea achieved 10.1 per cent average in annual GDP growth rate. In 2003–05, Korea exhibited moderate economic growth of 4–5 per cent due to stagnant domestic demand. In 2006, the real GDP growth rate was expected to be around 5 per cent, with private consumption growth around 3–5 per cent, equipment investment growth 5–9 per cent and exports another 8–12 per cent. The economy is expected to grow by 4.3 per cent per annum till 2020. Because of sluggish growth of inputs, the potential GDP growth rate is likely to decline for the next 15 years. Total factor productivity is expected to contribute more significantly.

## The Korean Economy

The Korean economy currently ranks number one in the world's shipbuilding industry, accounting for 41.2 per cent of the global shipbuilding production. The Korean steel industry has also emerged as an influential producer worldwide and ranks fifth largest in the world, producing 46.3 million tons of steel per year. It is also the world's No. 6 manufacturer of automobiles and produced 3.7 million cars in 2005.

In the 1940s, the country was predominantly agricultural, with little contribution from the industry sector. In the early 1960s, the government instituted sweeping economic reforms emphasizing exports and labour-intensive light industries. The emphasis shifted to light industry and consumer products in the following decades and then to heavy industry in the 1970s and 1980s. During the late 1990s and the 21st century, Korean high-tech industries became very competitive on the global market, especially in comparison with those of Japan and Taiwan, and dominated in international semiconductor chip production.

For the past four decades, rapid development of manufacturing industry has driven the economic growth of Korea. The share of the sector increased from 17.8 to 29 per cent during 1970 to 2004. Within this sector, heavy industry is the dominant one, with an almost 85 per cent share in 2004. The proportion of services industry has continuously increased from 44.7 per cent in 1970 to 55.5 per cent in 2004.

The South Korean economy has been heavily dependent on exports. In 2004, its export-GDP ratio stood at 39.6, against 20.5 for the world. In 2005, the volume of its total merchandise trade was around US$545 billion to US$285 billion in exports and US$260 billion in imports. Its foreign currency reserves stood at US$210 billion, the fourth largest in the world. The total volume of Korea's external trade amounted to 70 per cent of the country's gross domestic product.

The composition of Korea's export basket has undergone a major change over the years. While in 1960, most of the items exported belonged to the primary sector (iron ores, tungsten, raw silk), in 2005, it changed to the manufacturing and services sector. Semiconductors constitute the maximum share of Korea's merchandise exports (10.5%), followed by automobiles (10.4%), mobile phones (9.7%) and shipping vessels (6.2%). Concomitantly, the direction of trade has also undergone a shift. Thus, while in 1971, the USA was Korea's most important market with a 50% share, in 2005, China took over as the top destination with a 22% share, followed by the USA (14.5%), Japan (8.5%) and Hong Kong (5.5%). As for the import market,

Japan continues to rank first, though its share has declined from 40 to 18.5 per cent during 1971–2005. Although in South Korea, the import market has been liberalized in recent years, the agricultural market has remained largely protectionist due to serious disparities in the price of domestic agricultural products, such as rice, with the international market.

## KOREA'S TRADE POLICY AND THE IMPORTANCE OF FTAS

Korea's Trade Policy adopts a composite trade strategy. The principal trade policy objective is to build a "free and open economy" based on market principles to promote structural reform and efficiency. Raising exports is seen as a major growth engine for meeting the political target of doubling average per capita annual income to USU$20,000 (by 2010). Korea's "global leadership" trade and investment strategy in key sectors, such as motor vehicles, steel, and IT industries, is aimed at enhancing the economy's efficiency and achieving economic, including export-led, growth. Expanding high-technology industries and higher-value-added exports, and making Korea a Northeast Asia business and financial hub are high priorities of its trade policy.

One important policy change after the financial crisis was the country's keen interest in concluding free trade agreements with its trading partners. Following a wave of FTAs in the rest of Asia, Korea has also followed suit. Korea has already concluded bilateral FTAs with Chile in April 2004 and with Singapore in November 2004. It has already signed an FTA with the ASEAN member countries. Furthermore, it is currently having official discussions and joint studies with more than 20 countries, including Japan, EFTA-4 countries (Swiss, Norway, Iceland, Liechtenstein), Canada, Mexico, India, and MERCOSUR 4 countries (Brazil, Argentina, Uruguay, Paraguay), the USA, Russia and China.

Korea is pursuing FTAs so as to secure and expand foreign markets. It wants to promote competitiveness through structural reforms in industries. The strategies followed for FTAs are on a simultaneous multi-track basis. The Agreements are generally comprehensive high-level ones and are based on broad national support.

## KOREA-SINGAPORE BILATERAL ECONOMIC RELATIONS

The bilateral economic ties between the two countries are excellent. In 1995, total bilateral trade amounted to US$8.8 billion, which increased to

US$12.7 billion in 2005. Of this, while exports increased by 10 per cent to US$7.4 billion, imports increased by more than 100 per cent to US$5.3 billion during the same period. For Korea, while the major export commodities to Singapore include semiconductor, petroleum goods and automobiles, the major import commodities include electronic and electrical products. In 2005, Singapore was Korea's 9th largest trading partner. In exports, it ranks 7th and in imports its 11th.

During, 1968–2005, Korea invested US$1.2 billion in Singapore (202 projects), while it invested around US$122 million (24 projects) in 2005 alone. These were mainly in the retail sector, followed by manufacturing and services. Some recent cases of FDI from Korea to Singapore are that of SK Telecom (US$20 million), NESS Display (US$42 million), MAGINET (US$42 million), and SK energy (US$165 million). Singapore was the 8th largest foreign investor in Korea in 2005 with growing interests in areas like infrastructure, real estate, electronics, education and the banking sector.

During, 1968–2005, Singapore invested US$3.5 billion in Korea (620 projects), while it invested around US$390 million (90 projects) in 2005 alone. These are mainly in the retail sector, followed by manufacturing and services. Some recent cases of FDI from Singapore to Korea are that of Singapore Power (US$120 million), PSA (US$120 million), Hong Leong Group (US$210 million), and Temasek (US$400 million).

In the area of tourism, two-way visits have been increasing, with the number of Korean visitors reaching 291,811 in 2005. During 2003–05, Singapore visitor arrivals in Korea recorded a growth of 7.0 per cent, reaching 81,751. As against this, visitors from Korea to Singapore rose 54 per cent to touch 210,060 in 2005.

## THE KSFTA AND IMPLICATIONS FOR BILATERAL ECONOMIC COOPERATION

The KSFTA that came into force in March 2006 is a comprehensive and highly substantive agreement that aims to further enhance trade and investment flows between the two countries, bringing about a broadening and deepening of bilateral economic ties. The agreement goes beyond liberalization of trade in goods, services and investments to that of regulatory measures in the areas of competition policy, intellectual property protection, government procurement as well as other broad areas of economic cooperation, such as ICT, education and technology transfer.

The KSFTA is expected to help Korean companies in gaining a foothold into the Southeast Asian market. It is expected to build a strategic alliance with Singapore, the business hub of Southeast Asia. The FTA is expected to provide business opportunities for the opening of the services market and investment in both countries, especially in areas such as Architectural Services, Maritime Services, Real Estate Services and Financial Services. By allowing preferential access for imports from the Gaesong Industrial Complex (GIC) in North Korea, the KSFTA allows goods from GIC to be accorded the same status as Korean goods. As a result of this, nearly 15 companies in the GIC engaged in the exports of footwear, plastic goods, electronic parts, watches and apparel would enjoy preferential access to the Singapore market. Further, Mutual Recognition Agreements (MRAs) in the KSFTA are expected to reduce the cost and time of market access between the two countries, especially since IT related items, covered in the MRAs, account for 63 per cent of bilateral merchandise trade between the two countries.

The business sector in Korea has responded quite favourably to the KSFTA. In a survey by KITA, nearly 66 per cent of respondents viewed the KSFTA as being beneficial for expansion of bilateral economic relations between the two countries. Most companies in the survey emphasized that the KSFTA would provide them opportunities to lessen restrictions and open government procurement market in Singapore. The respondents believed that KSFTA would bring significant benefits to the trade sector in Korea, followed by logistics, finance, Information Technology, tourism, law, and healthcare.

## SUGGESTIONS FOR KOREA-SINGAPORE WIN-WIN COOPERATION THROUGH KSFTA

In the light of the above benefits form the KSFTA, the following suggestions are recommended to enhance the win-win cooperation:

1. *Build cooperation channels between private economic organizations.* The opening of KITA's Singapore office should be a great momentum for deepening cooperation between both countries.
2. *Utilize various forms of promotion activities to expand trade.* This can be done through promotions of various types of trade mission activities, including dispatching trade missions, inviting buyers, etc. Support for exhibitions and conventions can also be provided.
3. *Cooperate on strategic coalitions in IT & E-trade.* The IT technology of Korea and Global Network of Singapore can be merged. The

establishment of a joint e-trade platform of Korea and Singapore could also be useful.

4. *Promote Bilateral FDI.* Singapore should be encouraged to further increase its involvement in Korea's services industries. Singapore's strength of sourcing worldwide ability and Korea's strength in parts and material industries should be combined. Korea must also increase its investment in Singapore to use it as a financial and logistics hub.

# 4

## SALIENT FEATURES OF THE KSFTA AND EXPECTED BENEFITS FOR SINGAPORE

### INTRODUCTION

After seven rounds of negotiations beginning in 2003, the negotiations for the KSFTA were substantially concluded in November 2004 after trade ministers from both countries met on the fringe of the ASEAN Summit in Vientiane, Laos. The agreement is currently enforced since March 2006.

The KSFTA is a comprehensive and highly substantive agreement, which is WTO-consistent in principles and WTO-plus in commitments. It aims to further enhance trade and investment flows between the two countries, bringing about a broadening and deepening of bilateral economic ties. The agreement covers diverse areas ranging from trade in goods, services and investments to that of competition policy, intellectual property protection, government procurement and other broad areas of economic cooperation.

The remainder of this chapter examines the salient features of the KSFTA by examining its provisions in the above areas, and attempts to also analyse the possible benefits for Singapore businesses and consumers.

### TRADE IN GOODS

Under the KSFTA, 100 per cent of the Republic of Korea's (ROK's) exports will be allowed tariff-free entry into Singapore. Thus, Singapore will remove the remaining tariffs on alcoholic products immediately once the KSFTA comes into force.

Concomitantly, in case of Singapore's exports destined for Korea, up to 75 per cent of domestic exports valued at S$3 billion will enjoy immediate tariff elimination with the coming into force of the KSFTA. A further 14 per cent of domestic exports will also enjoy tariff-free access to the ROK market over the next ten years. Products ranging from freshwater ornamental fish to woven cotton fabrics as well as some of Singapore's exports from key sectors like electronics, electrical equipment and chemicals expected to benefit from these tariff concessions. Other sectors of importance to Singapore such as consumer electronics, precision engineering, biomedical sciences and chemicals are also covered by the FTA.

This will provide preferential access for Singapore exporters to the Korean market and is also expected to fuel intra-industry trade between the two countries, and thus potential beneficiaries will also be ROK companies with sourcing operations in Singapore for IT components, which they can export back to the ROK on preferential terms as inputs for their finished goods.

To cater to the ROK's domestic concerns, certain products which can pose a competitive challenge to ROK industry will have their tariffs phased out over a period of either five or ten years. This will provide enough time for the affected ROK industry sectors to gradually adjust to increased competition from Singaporean businesses. In addition, a small proportion of Singapore-origin products, which are regarded as highly sensitive to ROK industry and agriculture interests, will not be accorded preferential treatment.

In particular, although agriculture is a sensitive sector in the ROK, the inclusion of agricultural products was essential for Singapore given Singapore's keen interest in the processed food industry. For example, manufacturers of distinctively Singapore products such as three-in-one coffee mixes, chocolate confectionery, flour and tea concentrates will all get to benefit from the KSFTA.

Furthermore, to assuage the ROK's concerns over a possible deluge of Singapore imports that could cause injury to its domestic sectors, the FTA allows for the continued use of Anti-Dumping (AD) measures. The measures, however, have been tightened to ensure that no frivolous AD action can be taken by either party. Both parties are also allowed to take bilateral safeguard action for the first few years of the FTA and may continue to have recourse to the WTO safeguards agreement throughout the duration of the FTA.

Total tariff savings from the KSFTA for Singapore are estimated at S$75 million. These savings will be realized in three phases i.e. immediate elimination, over 5 years and over 10 years. It is estimated that there would be an immediate tariff savings of about S$25 million for Singapore upon entry into force of the KSFTA.

## Rules of Origin

Appropriate Rules of Origin (ROO) identifying the "nationality" of a product have been devised in the KSFTA that ensure that only ROK or Singaporean products enjoy the tariff preference negotiated under the Agreement. A product specific approach has been largely used to devise these rules. This approach was taken to cater to the specific needs of every industry, including industries of domestic concern to the ROK. This means that only goods manufactured in the ROK or Singapore will benefit from the FTA. Goods from third countries would not be able to pass off as Singapore-originating goods.

In addition, to ensure that there can be no unauthorized goods benefiting from the FTA, an ROK importer of a Singapore originating product also has to produce a Certificate of Origin (CO) issued by Singapore Customs as proof of its Singapore origin when claiming preference tariff treatment from the Korean Customs Authority. This tight system of certification will prevent circumvention of the KSFTA by products from third countries. To facilitate the benefits to the ROK's industries, the KSFTA also provides for the ROK to have a system of advance ruling that enables ROK importers and Singapore exporters to obtain clarification on the correct tariff classification and whether their products can be considered originating in Singapore prior to importation. This system offers greater certainty for the businesses and helps them to better plan their production and importation procedures.

One of the unique features in the KSFTA is that a selected list of products exported through the ROK has been accorded preferential treatment, regardless of the place of production. This list of products includes goods that will be produced in the Gaesong Industrial Complex (GIC), which is located in the Democratic People's Republic of Korea (DPRK), i.e. North Korea.[7] This provision takes into account unique manufacturing patterns in the Korean Peninsula, by allowing ROK enterprises with manufacturing facilities in industrial complexes such as the GIC to benefit from the FTA. Similarly, the ROK has taken into account Singapore's unique manufacturing patterns by providing recognition to outward processing under the ROO.

Similar provisions have also been incorporated for inclusion of Gaesong products in the ASEAN-Korea FTA.

The negotiators have taken utmost care to ensure that the above arrangement is WTO-consistent. Thus, the principle of non-discrimination is applied so that any country that chooses to export to Singapore through the ROK would benefit from this arrangement.

The ROK's Ministry of Foreign Affairs and Trade has clarified that goods from GIC would be labelled as "Made in North Korea". However, rules of origin for preferential treatment under the KSFTA would ensure that only the listed products manufactured in GIC under this arrangement are deemed as originating from the ROK. Since there is no cost saving from elimination of customs duties as all the goods in the list are already accorded zero duty by Singapore, there is no real benefit from the provision, even to the DPRK.

Further, the list of these products does have explicit provisions which prohibit the exportation of goods consistent with general and security exceptions under the WTO. In addition, both the ROK and Singapore have in place robust strategic goods control regimes. Under such regimes, permits will be required for the exportation of dual use goods, and the conveyance of these goods will also be closely monitored.

This arrangement in the KSFTA supports Singapore's overall stance towards economic engagement of the DPRK. Singapore has consistently expressed concern over the DPRK's decisions to reactivate its nuclear programme, to cease cooperation with the International Atomic Energy Agency, and to withdraw from the Non-Proliferation Treaty. Nevertheless, it also recognizes the importance of encouraging the DPRK to open up economically. Singapore therefore supports the efforts of the ROK to engage the DPRK,[8] and has been agreeable to create an opportunity to do so through the KSFTA.

## Trade Facilitation

The KSFTA has waived the requirement for a certificate of origin for low-value originating goods, thereby saving time and costs for importers and exporters. The Customs authorities on both sides are expected to further enhance the application of risk management to target high-risk goods and facilitate the clearance of low-risk consignments. In addition, they will also enhance transparency in regulation so that traders would be fully aware of the requirements and procedures in both countries.

## Mutual Recognition

By entering into mutual recognition agreements (MRAs) under the KSFTA, the ROK and Singapore stand to benefit from cost savings due to avoidance of duplicative testing. This will allow products to be cost competitive. Turn-around time for testing and certification will also be significantly reduced, enabling companies to market their goods faster.

A specific MRA of interest would be the Telecommunications MRA, where both the ROK and Singapore will recognize each other's telecommunications conformity assessment systems. Businesses from both countries would benefit from faster time-to-market and reduced costs. In particular, ROK companies exporting telecommunication equipment to Singapore will not need to submit their equipment for additional testing in Singapore so long as they are tested in the ROK by accredited test labs that are recognized by Singapore, and vice versa.

The ROK and Singapore have also agreed to inform each other of changes to their regulations. This will enable industry to make the necessary changes to its product designs, in order to fulfill new requirements ahead of the implementation of new regulations. It will also bring about market certainty as the risk of products being rejected by the regulators of the other FTA party will be greatly minimized.

## TRADE IN SERVICES

Under the KSFTA, service suppliers from both countries have been assured of fair and non-discriminatory treatment unless specifically exempted in writing — the so-called 'negative list' approach. This creates a level playing field for Singapore service suppliers as they will be treated as favourably as ROK service suppliers. There is a mechanism to lock in future liberalization of exempted measures, which creates certainty in the business climate since both governments are making a commitment to maintaining an open trading environment. These general measures are expected to spur bilateral trade in commercial services between the two countries, and also open up new investment opportunities for each other.

## Specific Sectoral Benefits for the ROK and Singapore

### Specific to the ROK

Professional Services:   The KSFTA provides ROK companies greater access to the Singaporean professional services market, particularly in the area of architectural, land surveying, engineering services and real estate services. As Singapore is home to more than 7,000 multinational companies, many of which have established their international or regional headquarters here, this growing list of international companies will present increasing opportunities for ROK's professional service providers.

<u>Construction Services</u>:   ROK companies will enjoy guaranteed access to Singapore's construction market, which had contracts worth $10 billion awarded in the year 2003. This will undoubtedly help to further boost ROK construction companies' presence in Singapore.

<u>Real Estate Services/Tourism</u>:   Under the KSFTA, ROK private developers will be allowed to develop specific plots of land on Sentosa and the Southern Islands of Singapore for tourism, commercial, residential and recreational purposes.

<u>Logistics Services</u>:   Singapore has been maintaining its international competitiveness and attractiveness as a logistics hub and supply chain management nerve centre in Asia even as competition stiffens. In 2003, investments in the logistics industry, including storage capacity expansion by Vopak and diversification by the Accord Group into new areas such as reverse logistics, are expected to generate $268 million in total business spending. Through the KSFTA, ROK logistics companies can now tap into this exciting landscape.

## Specific to Singapore

<u>Education Sector</u>:   The ROK education services sector is estimated to have a market size of US$84 billion in 2002, an increase of 10 per cent over the previous year. Within the Asian region, the ROK is one of the top five largest spenders in education, with expenditure on education taking up a large proportion of household expenditure. The KSFTA provides Singapore companies access to the ROK education services market, in particular, in the areas of language education, certified language programmes like TOEFL and TOEIC, corporate training and service quality programmes.

<u>Environmental Services</u>:   The ROK environmental services market is open in the areas of industrial waste treatment and refuse disposal services, environmental testing and assessment services, and recycling services. The ROK's environmental market has maintained a growth rate of over 15 per cent since 1995, which is higher than the world's average, and is projected to be worth approximately US$11 billion in the years between 2003 and

2005. This growing sector presents opportunities for Singapore's increasingly vibrant environmental services industry.

Services Incidental to Manufacturing:   Contract manufacturers are free to provide services that support the manufacture of machinery (office, computing, electrical), communications equipment, medical precision and optical instruments, rubber and plastics products.

Courier Services: Singapore service suppliers are given guaranteed access to the ROK's courier services sector. This certainty will provide an opportunity for Singapore and the ROK to complement each other as the South and North Asia hub for courier and logistics services. According to Euromonitor, the ROK's domestic market for courier services grew by about 17.1 per cent since 2002 to reach a value of US$1.68 billion in 2003.

## *Areas of Mutual Benefits*

Financial Services:   The KSFTA will allow the Singapore Exchange (SGX) and the Korean Stock Exchange (KSE) to work towards a SGX-KSE linkage that could enhance the liquidity pool in both markets and range of products available to investor.

ICT/E-Commerce:   The ROK and Singapore agreed under the KSFTA to explore cooperation in research and training activities that would enhance the development of ICT and in particular, e-commerce in both countries. Under this agreement, both countries also reaffirmed and strengthened their commitment to ensure that telecommunications companies operating or intending to operate in the other parties' market are accorded fair and non-discriminatory treatment, with specific obligations on the dominant suppliers in both countries. In addition to this greater market certainty, the agreement also provides operators a recourse mechanism to resolve telecommunications disputes through the relevant telecommunications regulatory bodies from each country.

## Movement of Natural Persons

Under the KSFTA, all citizens from the ROK will be granted 90 days stay on arrival in Singapore, an increase from the current 30 days; and intra-corporate transferees, traders and investors will be granted entry for a period of up to two years, which may be extended for subsequent periods up to a total of eight years. Further extensions beyond eight years may be possible. This will facilitate business interactions between Singapore and ROK companies and enhance possibilities for economic cooperation.

## INVESTMENT LIBERALIZATION AND INVESTOR PROTECTION

The KSFTA contains comprehensive commitments to protect investors and investments in both countries. Investors from ROK will be treated no differently from local investors in Singapore i.e. accorded National Treatment at both national and provincial levels. These provisions also apply to Singaporean investors in the ROK.

The KSFTA thus aims to foster an open environment for cross-border investment, minimize restrictions and spell out clearly any market access restrictions. It is expected that this would give investments from Singapore to the ROK and vice-versa, greater protection and certainty in their business operations.

The investment provisions under the KSFTA agreement also contain provisions allowing the right to freely transfer funds relating to this investment. Both sides have also agreed not take over the assets of the company unreasonably without proper compensation. Should an aggrieved investor feel that the ROK or Singapore has acted in breach of its obligations under the FTA, it can take the ROK or the Singapore government to an international arbitration tribunal. This right of the investor is in addition to and independent of any other contractual rights.

Significantly, both sides have agreed not to impose a list of restrictive conditions relating to the establishment and management of investments, as well as to the granting of incentives. This is a strong commitment found in the most forward-looking of FTAs.

### Intellectual Property Protection

Under the KSFTA, there will be mutual assurance that, in the field of Intellectual Property, there is adequate and effective protection in both the ROK and Singapore by way of intellectual property rights and enforcement practices that are consistent with internationally recognized standards. The KSFTA has also proposed strategic links with the ROK in the form of cooperation on several key areas in Intellectual Property, for example, patent technology and licensing, and in the education, promotion and awareness of Intellectual Property and Intellectual Property Rights.

The appointment of the Korea Intellectual Property Office (KIPO) as an International Search Authority (ISA) and International Patents and Examination Authority (IPEA) provides applicants in Singapore with the added option of choosing the Korean Intellectual Property Office (in addition to the existing options of the European Patent Office and the Australian Patent Office) as the office to perform the search and examination when they file an international patent application under the Patent Cooperation Treaty system.

Singapore has also appointed the Korean Intellectual Property Office as a Prescribed Patent Office (PPO). This will result in time and cost savings for patent applications in Singapore by ROK individuals and businesses, making Singapore a highly attractive location for ROK's knowledge-based R&D investments.

## GOVERNMENT PROCUREMENT

Although Singapore already benefits from the government procurement market of the ROK under the WTO-Agreement for Government Procurement (GPA), the KSFTA will provide increased benefits. For example, the threshold of GP projects has been reduced from S$307,000 to S$236,000, allowing more companies to benefit from government procurement opportunities. ROK firms will be treated on equal terms as Singaporean firms in supplying such goods and services, and vice-versa.

## COMPETITION POLICY

The KSFTA Competition Chapter puts in place a framework for the ROK and Singapore to promote competition by addressing anti-competitive practices in their respective territory, adopting and enforcing such measures as they deem appropriate and effective to counter such practices. Among these, both countries are to ensure that their respective laws on competition are equally applied to all businesses in their territory.

The Chapter also provides that both countries can enter into consultations on competition matters, including the elimination of particular anti-competitive practices that affect trade or investment between the Parties. Both countries recognize the importance of cooperation and coordination between their competition authorities for effective competition law enforcement. To this end, there is also provision on consulting on a separate arrangement between the competition authorities regarding such cooperation and coordination. These provisions would help provide a level-playing field for new companies entering the market from both countries.

## BROADER AREAS OF ECONOMIC COOPERATION

The Cooperation Chapter in the KSFTA offers benefits for both countries in a wide range of areas. Memorandum of Understandings (MOUs) signed in the areas of Trade and Investment Promotion, Broadcasting, Film and Games, Human Resource Management and Development, and Environment will create more avenues for increased cooperation and exchange of knowledge in the respective areas. Particularly noteworthy areas include:

Broadcasting:  The MOU between the Media Development Authority (MDA) and the Korea Broadcasting Commission (KBC) would allow various forms of cooperation, such as the co-production of country videos to increase awareness of both countries and the KSFTA.

Film and Games:  The MOU would allow Singapore to learn from the advanced knowledge the ROK possesses in this area, such as through training and attachment programmes, and the co-production of films by interested parties in both countries.

Human Resource Management and Development: The MOU would help the ROK gain knowledge of the People's Developer Standard adopted in many Ministries in Singapore.

Environment:  The MOU signed between the Environment Ministries of both countries would encourage the exchange of CNG technology.

Such cooperative efforts will enable both countries to develop closer economic ties beyond conventional trade and investment liberalization. Moving forward, the KSFTA will be a key platform to bring bilateral economic relations to a higher plane.

### Dispute Settlement and Consultation

Under the KSFTA, the ROK and Singapore have negotiated a comprehensive set of dispute settlement procedures, to ensure that if differences arise as to the interpretation or the implementation of rights and obligations under the Agreement, a predictable, efficient and effective framework is in place to resolve the dispute as quickly as possible.

# 5

## SINGAPORE-KOREA BUSINESS LINKAGES POST-KSFTA AND IMPLEMENTION

This chapter[9] aims to analyse some of emerging trends in Singapore's businesses entering Korea post-KSFTA, highlighting the success of specific Singapore companies that have benefited from the KSFTA. The chapter also highlights some of the mechanisms through which the KSFTA implementation is being monitored, focusing on the facilitative role played by International Enterprise (IE) Singapore in this process.

### POST KSFTA SCENARIO AND BUSINESS ACTIVITIES

While Singapore companies in the real estate and food services were been particularly active in Korea even prior to the KSFTA, IE Singapore has been actively assisting Singapore companies in their ventures to and expansion in Korea by playing the facilitator's role and providing market know-how. In 2006, IE led four missions to Korea in sectors such as Infocomm Technology (ICT), Electronics and Precision Engineering (EPE), Lifestyle Services and Business Services. These missions were aimed at helping companies to explore the market and meet up with potential Korean partners. IE Singapore has planned another four out-going missions to Korea this year. It also signed a Memorandum of Understanding with the Korea-Trade Investment Promotion Agency (KOTRA) to foster greater trade and investment between the two countries through collaborative activities. Two key Korean agencies, the Korea International Trade Association (KITA) and the Small Business Corporation (SBC), established representative offices in Singapore in 2006.

According to the Korea International Trade Association, figures of growth rates of exports and imports of some major items of trade between Korea and Singapore have revealed that products such as oil and chemicals on which tariff reductions were undertaken by Korea in the KSFTA have led to expansion of imports of these products from Singapore 10 months after the KSFTA took effect, compared to its growth 10 months before the agreement was implemented. On the export side, semiconductors and steel slabs have seen a comparatively higher growth rate from Korea to Singapore in the post-KSFTA period.[10]

It is also noted that beyond trade and investment relations, people and cultural flows are also important in forging stronger bilateral relations. Singapore welcomed 454,666 Korean visitors in 2006. Concomitantly, Korea too has become popular tourist destinations for Singapore tourists for shopping, skiing and visits to the 大长今 (Dae Jang Geum) filming site. Over 70,000 Singaporeans visited Korea in 2006.[11]

## KSFTA Success Case: Aalst Chocolate

One of the first success stories of the KSFTA enabling more Singapore-based companies to expand their market share in Korea, was that of *Aalst Chocolate*. A recent interview quoted President and Chief Executive Officer of *Aalst Chocolate*, Mr Richard Lee,

> After the KSFTA has been signed, we received many enquiries from potential Korean customers. Knowing that products from Singapore will be more price-competitive via tariff reduction; and goods will be received faster because custom procedures have been streamlined; Korean customers are much more open to collaborate with suppliers in Singapore. In fact, import duties for chocolate, which have been reduced from eight per cent to 5.3 per cent in 2007, will be further reduced gradually over the next four years until they are eliminated in 2011.

This is an indication that the KSFTA has been successful in expanding Singapore's market access in Korea, and it has already generated positive expectations of a further boost in trade and investment between businesses from both countries.

## MONITORING IMPLEMENTATION OF KSFTA AND THE ROLE OF IE SINGAPORE

IE Singapore is playing a critical role in monitoring implementation of the KSFTA from the Singapore side, assisting Singapore companies in their business ventures to and expansion in Korea. IE Singapore led four missions to Korea in 2006 in the Infocomm Technology (ICT), Electronic and Precision Engineering (EPE), Business Services, and Lifestyle Services. In 2007, as mentioned earlier, IE Singapore has planned another four out-going missions to Korea to help companies explore the market and meet up with potential Korean partners. It also organizes business matching sessions with Korean companies interested in setting up their businesses or expanding operations in Singapore.

Following the KSFTA, IE Singapore signed a Memorandum of Understanding (MOU) with KOTRA in June 2006 to promote strategic alliances between Singapore-based and Korean companies, as well as to assist them in market expansion and development of market knowledge and networks. One of the notable successes in fostering investment collaboration between Singapore and Korean companies by IE Singapore has been that of Singapore-based spa operator SpaCare forming a joint alliance with Korean conglomerate Daesun Group to build multiple spas in Korea over 2007–09.

## OPPORTUNITIES FOR SINGAPORE-KOREA BUSINESS COLLABORATION POST-KSFTA

As noted by Singapore's Minister for Trade and Industry in a recent speech,[12] Korea is attractive to Singapore businesses in a number of ways. Korea has a market of around 48 million. Its relatively high affluence level, particularly in Seoul, for instance, makes up an interesting and sizeable market for products and services. Secondly, Korea is located within a 2-hour flight from Japan and China — two of the world's largest economies. In sectors such as logistics and manufacturing, Korea can be a good spring board for serving Japan and northeast China. Already 12 major Singapore companies are operating in Korea in a diverse range of business activities (Table 5.1).

The same speech notes that Singapore is attractive to many Korean companies as a gateway to Southeast Asia, South Asia and the Middle East. There are currently 489 registered companies from Korea in Singapore, engaging in activities such as international trading, logistics &

**TABLE 5.1**
**Major Singapore Business Activities in Korea**

| No. | Company | Business Activities in Korea |
|---|---|---|
| 1. | Temasek Holdings | Having successfully applied to buy an additional 6.39 per cent stake in the Korea's fourth-largest lender, Hana Bank, currently holds almost 10 per cent stake in the bank. Temasek's request had to be approved by the Ministry of Finance and Economy of Korea as foreign companies are currently not allowed to buy more than 4 per cent of a domestic bank without clearance. |
| 2. | BeXcom | Formed an alliance with Hyundai Corp to establish an e-Trading hub in Korea. |
| 3. | IDA and Korea Thrunet | Had collaboration in content development. |
| 4. | SingTel | Set up representative offices in Seoul. SingTel Korea was incorporated as a full subsidiary in 2000, selling virtual private network services (VPN). |
| 5. | Sesami | Set up its representative office for e-commerce services at Teheran Valley (Korean version of Silicon Valley) in December 2000. It also formed a strategic alliance with Samsung Imarket Korea for procurement services for corporate accounts in 2002. |
| 6. | Singapore Power | Acquired a US$160 million power plant, and among others, a power generation facility from Samsung General Chemicals. Singapore Power also acquired a US$30 million water treatment facility in Korea. |
| 7. | Fraser & Neave | Set up a serviced apartment in Seoul in a US$34 million partnership with Rodamco Insa (a JV between Rodamco and F&N). |

**TABLE 5.1** (*continued*)

| No. | Company | Business Activities in Korea |
|---|---|---|
| 8. | Sembcorp Logistics | (Acquired by Australia TOLL Group in 2006), formed a JV with Kukbo from S. Korea to provide 3PL services to MNCs and Korean conglomerates based in North Asia. |
| 9. | OSIM's | First franchise store in Seoul, Korea was opened in August 2004. |
| 10. | GIC Real Estate Pte Ltd (GIC RE) | Through its affiliate, acquired a portfolio of two prime office buildings (Kolon Building and Mookyo Building) in the heart of the Seoul CBD from affiliates of Morgan Stanley Properties Korea Limited in January 2004. These two 15 storey freehold office buildings are close to major financial, commercial and government buildings, and are next to the Seoul Financial Centre owned by GIC RE. |
| 11. | Ya Kun Kaya Toast | Opened two franchise stores in Korea. Located in the upmarket end of Seoul, Ya Kun has plans to open more franchise stores in Seoul. |
| 12. | Crystal Jade Restaurants | Opened its first Chinese restaurant in Seoul in July 2005. |

*Source*: http://www.iesingapore.gov.sg/wps/wcm/connect/IE+Alerts?id=e5e0570a16836 5b&PageDesign=IE+Newsletter+Content+Presentation+Template

transport, and construction & engineering. All the major Korean *chaebol* are represented in Singapore. Notably, Samsung Asia operates its Asia Pacific hub for procurement, logistics and administrative functions here. Korean Airlines has also recently designated Singapore as a regional headquarters for Asia. In addition, companies such as SK Corporation, Hyosung and Hanjin use Singapore for international trading, shipping and procurement operations. In this way Singapore can be a gateway for Korean companies to venture into ASEAN and beyond, post KSFTA.

Two areas identified by IE Singapore that would offer significant potential for business expansion between the two countries post-KSFTA would be that of Infocomm Technology and Lifestyle services. It is noted by IE Singapore that Singapore players with niche technologies in software development and game developers can team up with the Korean counterparts to tap into the international market. Partnerships are essential as having the right partner helps the company to penetrate the markets more effectively. Therefore, it is working with the Infocomm Development Authority of Singapore as well as the Games Exchange Alliance to profile Singapore's games developers, especially to Korean companies, and led the first ICT mission to Korea in 2006, post-KSFTA.

In the area of lifestyle services, viz. spa services, rising affluence in Korea offers a significant consumer market for Singapore-based companies. Singapore operators have been taking up space for such services in shopping malls and hotels in Korea to cater to busy office workers. Offering services for rejuvenation and well-being, Singapore operators provide a niche and complementary role in the Korean spa market, which is rooted in hot spring and bath culture. Singapore companies can also add value in partnering with Korean counterparts through their strength in spa management.

## FUTURE PROSPECTS

In the light of the ongoing efforts by IE Singapore in implementation and significant expansion in business activities envisaged in the post-KSFTA period, the future prospects of strengthening economic linkages through the KSFTA appear bright. However, this would require encouraging more Korean companies to forge partnerships with Singapore based businesses to develop the markets of Southeast Asia and South Asia. Korean companies are yet to take advantage of a strong network of business linkages and free trade agreements of Singapore to explore opportunities in various sectors. In particular, they could consider investing in the electronics sector. Singapore has a comprehensive range of electronics and precision-engineering companies that can support high-end manufacturing wafer fabrication and IC design operations, as in case of Korea.

Further, Korean petrochemical companies can similarly leverage on this platform to penetrate third-country markets in the region. Singapore already offers a cost-competitive and synergistic environment for some of the world's leading petroleum, petrochemical and specialty chemicals giants, including ExxonMobil, Shell and Sumitomo. As an example, Korean company SK Energy Asia is one of the largest traders in Singapore, with a turnover of US$12 billion. In January 2005, SK Corporation announced its plans to invest in a US$10 million (5.3 million barrel) petroleum storage facility on Jurong Island. This marks the first time that a major Asian refiner has taken a direct stake in an independent storage in Singapore. SK Energy Asia should consider downstream manufacturing in Singapore in the near future, by taking advantage of the KSFTA. Finally, Korean companies should also tap the resources of the Korea Trade and Investment Promotion Agency (KOTRA), the Korea International Trade Agency (KITA) and the Korea Small Business Corporation (SBC) that now have representative offices in Singapore. These institutions provide the supporting business infrastructure to facilitate information flow and business linkages in the post-KSFTA period.

It is important to note that the KSFTA currently covers 74 per cent of Singapore's exports to Korea. Efforts need to be taken to continuously monitor the progress of the KSFTA and try to increase this coverage to 90 per cent as and when the KSFTA is reviewed.[13] This would ensure that bilateral trade and investment linkages between the two countries continue to strengthen after the enforcement of the KSFTA.

This chapter thus emphasizes that although it is perhaps too early to gauge the impact of the KSFTA, a modest success is already evident. Efforts of IE Singapore and its Korean counterparts will further ensure that the KSFTA is successfully implemented, and utilized by businesses in both countries to expand bilateral economic linkages to a higher level.

# 6

# CONCLUDING REMARKS

The KSFTA, Korea's first comprehensive bilateral FTA, will not only provide significant economic benefits for Singapore, but also provide a framework for building a strong strategic and economic partnership between Korea and ASEAN countries. It is therefore designed to be a building block in the process of community-building efforts towards an East Asian Community in the long run. The efforts by IE Singapore to expand business linkages after the enforcement of the KSFTA offer valuable lessons in the implementation of FTAs.

However, it is important to note that the KSFTA, while being an important constituent of this process, will need to be supported by similar ongoing efforts by Korea and other ASEAN members. These countries would therefore need to strive towards negotiating comprehensive bilateral FTAs that generate substantial and concrete economic benefits in not just commodity trade and service transactions, but in reducing transaction costs and in bringing about greater transparency and private-sector participation in the business environment in Asia. Towards this end, FTAs do serve as an important regional community-building tool towards adjusting to the forces of globalization. However, while negotiating such agreements, important domestic reforms to boost competitiveness would need to be addressed simultaneously to generate a win-win situation for all parties involved in such negotiations.[14] This would be particularly crucial for middle- and lower-income developing countries in Asia that do not possess enough bargaining power during negotiations to generate substantial economic benefits through an FTA.

# NOTES

The author would like to thank the Ministry of Trade and Industry (MTI), and International Enterprise (IE) Singapore for their support and encouragement in publishing this monograph. The author also thanks his colleague Dr Rahul Sen for his inputs to this study, particularly in facilitating the preparation of the draft. The usual disclaimer applies.

[1]  See http://www.iesingapore.gov.sg/wps/portal/FTA for further details on Singapore's FTAs.

[2]  This chapter occasionally draws on the Joint Study Group Report on the Korea-Singapore FTA.

[3]  Cumulative figures are from 1980 to 2002 for Korea's investments to Singapore and from 1962 to 2002 for Singapore's investments to Korea.

[4]  The SMBA was established for efficient and effective implementation of SME-related policies and on-the-spot support of regional SMEs, through various initiatives such as the analysis of industry trends, promotion of start-up venture companies including the selection of industrial sites, development of technology, and cooperation promotion between local government offices and related local SMEs.

[5]  The Korea Venture Acceleration Centre (KVAC) was jointly founded by the EDB and Korea's Small and Medium Business Administration to help attract and support Korean companies to Singapore.

[6]  This chapter is adapted from a presentation by Dr Hyun Oh-Seok made at the KSFTA Conference organized by SBF on 14 March 2006. The author would like to thank him for this valuable contribution.

[7]  The GIC was established in 2003 as part of South Korea's "Sunshine Policy" towards the North. It is estimated that when completed, the GIC will create 150,000 jobs and produce goods worth US$14.5 billion a year.

[8]  This is reiterated in Singapore's Foreign Minister BG George Yeo's recent visit to Gaesong, wherein in his entry in the Gaesong guestbook he wished the Korean people success in developing the GIC as a base for "eventual reunification".

[9]  Much of the discussion in this chapter is based on the author's discussions with IE Singapore officials Mr Thian Tai Chew and Mr Jad Ng. The

authors would like to express their thanks for this important contribution to this study.

[10] See "*Korea-Singapore Trade Has Surged Since FTA Took Effect (Mar 2, 2007)*" at http://english.mofe.go.kr/news/pressrelease_view.php?sect=news_press&pmode=&cat=&sn=5074&page=1&SK=ALL&SW=investment

[11] This was observed in the Keynote Address by Mr Lee Yi Shyan, Minister of State for Trade and Industry, Singapore, at the "Bridging Partnerships between Korea and Singapore" Conference, 30 March 2007.

[12] Ibid.

[13] Ibid.

[14] See R. Sally and R. Sen, "Whither Trade Policies in Southeast Asia? The Wider Asian and Global Context", *ASEAN Economic Bulletin* 22, no. 1 (2005): 92–115.

# REFERENCES

Export-Import Bank of Korea. Foreign Investment Statistics available at http://www. koreaexim.go.kr/en/fdi/m02/s04_01.jsp. Accessed in 2007.

International Enterprise (IE) Singapore. *Singapore Trade Statistics*, Singapore. International Enterprises, 2007.

Korea Customs Service. *Statistical Yearbook of Foreign Trade*. Seoul: Korea Customs Service, 2003.

Korea-Singapore FTA Joint Study Group. 2003.

Liang, Margaret. "Singapore's Trade Policies: Priorities and Options". *ASEAN Economic Bulletin* 22, no. 1 (2005): 49–59.

Sally, Razeen and Rahul Sen. "Whither Trade Policies in Southeast Asia? The Wider Asian and Global Context". *ASEAN Economic Bulletin* 22, no. 1 (2005): 92–115.

World Trade Organization (WTO). *International Trade Statistics 2006*. Geneva: WTO, 2006.

# APPENDIX

## FREE TRADE AGREEMENT BETWEEN THE GOVERNMENT OF THE REPUBLIC OF KOREA AND THE GOVERNMENT OF THE REPUBLIC OF SINGAPORE

The Government of the Republic of Korea ("Korea") and the Government of the Republic of Singapore ("Singapore"), hereinafter referred to as "the Parties";

Conscious of their bonds of longstanding friendship and strong trade and investment relationship;

Recalling the establishment of a Joint Study Group to examine the benefits of a Free Trade Agreement between the Government of the Republic of Korea and the Government of the Republic of Singapore ("Korea-Singapore FTA") in October 2002;

Desiring to adopt the recommendations in the Joint Study Group Report that the Parties proceed to negotiate the Korea-Singapore FTA, and that the Joint Study Group Report should serve as a framework for negotiations on the FTA;

Reaffirming their commitment to securing trade liberalisation and an outward-looking approach to trade and investment;

Convinced that their economic integration would generate larger economies of scale, provide greater work opportunities, and enhance transparency for economic activities for their businesses as well as for other businesses in Asia;

Sharing the belief that a free trade agreement between the Parties would improve their attractiveness to capital and human resources, and create larger and new markets, to expand trade and investment not only between them but also in the region;

Affirming their commitment to fostering the development of open market economy in Asia, and to encouraging economic integration of Asian economies in order to further the liberalisation of trade and investment in the region;

Reaffirming that this Agreement shall contribute to the expansion and development of world trade under the multilateral trading system embodied in the Marrakesh Agreement Establishing the World Trade Organization ("the WTO Agreement");

Building on their respective rights and obligations under the WTO Agreement and other multilateral, regional and bilateral instruments of co-operation; and

Resolved to promote reciprocal trade and investment, and to avoid circumvention of benefits of regional trade integration, through the establishment of clear and mutually advantageous trade rules, and industry as well as regulatory co-operation;

HAVE AGREED as follows:

## CHAPTER 1
## GENERAL PROVISIONS


ARTICLE **1.1**: ESTABLISHMENT OF FREE TRADE AREA

The Parties to this Agreement, consistent with Article XXIV of GATT 1994 and Article V of GATS, hereby establish a free trade area in accordance with the provisions of this Agreement.


ARTICLE **1.2**: OBJECTIVES

The objectives of this Agreement, as elaborated more specifically through its principles and rules, including national treatment, most-favoured-nation treatment and transparency, are to:

(a) liberalise and facilitate trade in goods and services and expand investment between the Parties;
(b) establish a co-operative framework for strengthening the economic relations between the Parties;
(c) establish a framework conducive for a more favourable environment for their businesses and promote conditions of fair competition in the free trade area;
(d) establish a framework of transparent rules to govern trade and investment between the Parties;
(e) create effective procedures for the implementation and application of this Agreement; and
(f) establish a framework for further regional and multilateral co-operation to expand and enhance the benefits of this Agreement throughout Asia, and thereby, to encourage economic integration of Asian economies.


ARTICLE **1.3**: RELATION TO OTHER AGREEMENTS

1. The Parties reaffirm their existing rights and obligations with respect to each other under existing bilateral and multilateral agreements to which both Parties are party, including the WTO Agreement.

2. In the event of any inconsistency between this Agreement and other agreements to which both Parties are party, the Parties shall immediately consult with each other with a view to finding a mutually satisfactory solution, taking into consideration general principles of international law.

3.    Notwithstanding paragraph 2, if this Agreement explicitly contains provisions regarding such inconsistency as indicated in paragraph 2, those provisions shall apply.

### ARTICLE 1.4: REFERENCE OO OTHER AGREEMENTS

1.    For the purposes of this Agreement, any reference to articles in GATT 1994 or GATS includes the interpretative notes, where applicable.

2.    Any reference in this Agreement to any other treaty or international agreement shall be made in the same terms to its successor treaty or international agreement to which both Parties are party.

## CHAPTER 2
## GENERAL DEFINITIONS

For the purposes of this Agreement, unless otherwise specified:

**Agreement** means this free trade agreement between the Parties;

**APEC** means the Asia-Pacific Economic Co-operation;

**citizen** means:

(a) with respect to Korea, a Korean as defined in Article 2 of the Constitution of the Republic of Korea and its domestic laws; and
(b) with respect to Singapore, any person who is a citizen within the meaning of its Constitution and domestic laws;

**Custom Valuation Agreement** means the Agreement on Implementation of Article VII of the General Agreement on Tariff and Trade 1994, which is part of the WTO Agreement;

**days** means calendar days including weekends and holidays;

**enterprise** means any corporation, company, association, partnership, trust, joint venture, sole-proprietorship or other legally recognised entity that is duly incorporated, constituted, set up, or otherwise duly organised under the law of a Party, including branches, regardless of whether or not the entity is organised for pecuniary gain, privately or otherwise owned, or organised with limited or unlimited liability;
**existing** means in effect at the time of entry into force of this Agreement;

**GATS** means the General Agreement on Trade in Services, which is a part of the WTO Agreement;

**GATT 1994** means the General Agreement on Tariffs and Trade 1994, which is a part of the WTO Agreement;

**Generally Accepted Accounting Principles** means the recognised consensus or substantial authoritative support in the territory of a Party with respect to the recording of revenues, expenses, costs, assets and liabilities, the disclosure of information and the preparation of financial statements. These standards may encompass broad guidelines of general application as well as detailed standards, practices and procedures;

**Harmonized System (HS)** means the Harmonized Commodity Description and Coding System, including its General Rules of Interpretation, Section Notes and Chapter Notes;

**measure** means any law, regulation, procedure or administrative action, requirement or practice;

**national** means a natural person who is a citizen or permanent resident of a Party;

**permanent resident** means any person who has the right of permanent residence in the territory of a Party;

**person** means a natural person or an enterprise;

**person of a Party** means a national or an enterprise of a Party;
territory means:

(a) with respect to Korea, the land, maritime, and air space under its sovereignty, and those maritime areas, including the seabed and subsoil adjacent to the outer limit of the territorial sea over which it exercises sovereign rights or jurisdiction in accordance with international law and its domestic law; and

(b) with respect to Singapore, its land territory and airspace above in accordance with international law, internal waters and territorial sea as well as the maritime zones beyond the territorial sea, including the seabed and subsoil, over which the Republic of Singapore exercises sovereign rights or jurisdiction under its national laws and international law for the purpose of exploration and exploitation of the natural resources of such areas; and

**WTO Agreement** means the Marrakesh Agreement Establishing the World Trade Organization, done on April 15, 1994.

## CHAPTER 3
## NATIONAL TREATMENT AND MARKET ACCESS FOR GOODS

ARTICLE 3.1: DEFINITION

For the purposes of this Chapter:

**other duties or charges** means any duty or charge of any kind, except customs duty, imposed on or in connection with the importation of goods of the other Party, but does not include any:

(a) duty imposed pursuant to Chapter 6 (Trade Remedies);
(b) charge equivalent to an internal tax imposed consistently with Article III: 2 of GATT 1994;
(c) fee or other charge in connection with importation commensurate with the cost of services rendered;
(d) premium offered or collected on an imported good arising out of any tendering system in respect of the administration of quantitative import restrictions, tariff rate quotas or tariff preference levels; or
(e) duty imposed pursuant to Article 5 of the WTO Agreement on Agriculture.

ARTICLE 3.2: SCOPE AND COVERAGE

This Chapter shall be applied to the trade in goods between the Parties.

ARTICLE 3.3: NATIONAL TREATMENT

Each Party shall accord national treatment to the goods of the other Party in accordance with Article III of GATT 1994. To this end, Article III of GATT 1994 is incorporated into and made part of this Agreement.

ARTICLE 3.4: TARIFF ELIMINATION

1.  Except as otherwise provided in this Agreement, each Party shall progressively eliminate its customs duties and other duties or charges on originating goods of the other Party in accordance with its Tariff Elimination Schedule set out in Annex 3A.

2.  Upon request of a Party, the Parties shall consult to consider accelerating the elimination of customs duties as set out in their Tariff Elimination Schedules or incorporating into one Party's Tariff Elimination Schedule goods that are not subject

to the Tariff Elimination Schedule. An agreement by the Parties to accelerate the elimination of customs duties on an originating good or to include a good in the Tariff Elimination Schedule shall supersede any duty rate or staging category determined pursuant to their Tariff Elimination Schedules for such good, shall be treated as an amendment to Annex 3A and shall enter into force in accordance with the procedure under Article 22.4.

### ARTICLE 3.5: CUSTOMS VALUATION

The Parties shall apply Article VII of GATT 1994 and the provisions of Part I of the Customs Valuation Agreement for the purposes of determining the customs value of goods traded between the Parties.

### ARTICLE 3.6: EXPORT DUTY

Neither Party shall adopt or maintain any duties on goods exported from its territory into the territory of the other Party.

### ARTICLE 3.7: GOODS RE-ENTERED AFTER REPAIR OR PROCESS

In accordance with its domestic laws and regulations, each Party may exempt or reduce a customs duty to a good, regardless of its origin, that re-enters its territory after that good has been exported or if it was under a temporary exit from its territory to the territory of the other Party for repair or process, regardless of whether such repair or process could be performed in its territory.

### ARTICLE 3.8: IMPORT AND EXPORT RESTRICTIONS

1.   Neither Party may adopt or maintain any prohibition or restriction on the importation of any good of the other Party or on the exportation or sale for export of any good destined for the territory of the other Party, except in accordance with rights and obligations under the WTO Agreement, or except as otherwise provided in this Agreement.

2.   In the event that a Party adopts or maintains a prohibition or restriction on the importation of a good from a non-Party, nothing in this Agreement shall be construed to prevent the Party from limiting or prohibiting the importation from the territory of the other Party of such a good of that non-Party.

3.   In the event that a Party adopts or maintains a prohibition or restriction on the importation of a good from a non-Party, the Parties, upon request of the other

Party, shall consult with a view to avoiding undue interference with or distortion of pricing, marketing and distribution arrangements in the other Party.

### ARTICLE 3.9: CUSTOMS USER FEES

Customs user fees shall be limited in amount to the approximate cost of services rendered and shall not represent an indirect protection for domestic products or a taxation of imports or exports for fiscal purposes. They shall be based on specific rates that correspond to the real value of the service rendered.

### ARTICLE 3.10: BALANCE OF PAYMENT EXCEPTION

1.   Where a Party is in serious balance of payments and external financial difficulties or threat thereof, it may, in accordance with GATT 1994 and the Understanding on the Balance-of-Payments Provisions of GATT 1994, adopt restrictive import measures. The relevant provisions of GATT 1994 and the Understanding on the Balance-of-Payments Provisions of GATT 1994 are hereby incorporated into and made part of the Agreement.

2.   The Party introducing a measure under this Article shall promptly notify the other Party.

## CHAPTER 4
## RULES OF ORIGIN

ARTICLE 4.1: DEFINITIONS

For the purposes of this Chapter:

**customs value** means:

    (a)  the price actually paid or payable for a good or material with respect to a transaction of the seller of the good, pursuant to the principles of Article 1 of the Customs Valuation Agreement, adjusted in accordance with Article 8 of the Customs Valuation Agreement; or

    (b)  in the event that there is no such value or such value of the good is unascertainable, the value determined in accordance with Articles 2 through 7 of the Customs Valuation Agreement;

**F.O.B.** means free on board value of a good payable by the buyer to the seller, regardless of the mode of transportation, not including any internal excise taxes reduced, exempted, or repaid when the good is exported;

**fungible goods or materials** means goods or materials that are interchangeable for commercial purposes and whose properties are essentially identical;

**good** means any merchandise, product, article or material;

**goods wholly obtained or produced entirely in the territory of one or both of the Parties** means:

    (a)  mineral goods extracted there;

    (b)  plants and plant products grown and harvested, picked or gathered there;

    (c)  live animals born and raised there;

    (d)  goods obtained from hunting or trapping conducted there;

    (e)  goods obtained from fishing within the outer limit of the territorial sea of one or both of the parties;

    (f)  products of sea-fishing and other products taken from the sea outside of the territorial sea of one or both of the Parties by vessels registered or recorded with a Party and flying its flag;

    (g)  goods produced on board factory ships from the goods referred to in paragraph (f), provided such factory ships are registered or recorded with one of the Parties and flying its flag;

(h)  goods taken by a Party or a person of a Party from the seabed or beneath the seabed outside territorial waters, provided that the Party has rights to exploit such seabed;

(i)  goods taken from outer space, provided that they are obtained by a Party or a person of a Party and not processed in the territory of a non-Party;

(j)  waste and scrap derived from:

(i)  production there; or

(ii)  used goods collected there, provided that such goods are fit only for the recovery of raw materials; and

(k)  goods produced in the territory of one or both of the Parties exclusively from goods referred to in paragraphs (a), (b), (c), (d), (e), (f), (g), (h), (i) and (j), or from their derivatives, at any stage of production;

**intermediate material** means a material that is self-produced and used in the production of a good, and designated pursuant to Article 4.7;

**material** means a good that is used in the production of another good and physically incorporated into the good;

**non-originating good or non-originating material** means a good or material that does not qualify as originating under this Chapter;

**originating material** means a material that qualifies as originating under Article 4.2;

**packing materials and containers for shipment** means goods used to protect a good during its transportation, different from those containers or materials used for its individual sale;

**producer** means a person who grows, mines, raises, harvests, fishes, reproduces and breeds, traps, hunts, manufactures, processes, assembles or disassembles a good;

**production** means method of obtaining goods including growing, raising, mining, harvesting, fishing, reproducing and breeding, trapping, hunting, manufacturing, processing, assembling or disassembling a good;

**used** means used or consumed in the production of goods; and

**value of materials** means:

(a)  except in the case of packing materials and containers for shipment, for the purposes of calculating the regional value content of a good and for the purposes of applying the De Minimis rule, the value of a material that is used in the production of a good shall:

(i)   for a material that is imported by the producer of the good, be the customs value of the material with respect to the importation including the costs of freight, insurance, packing and all other costs incurred in the international shipment of that material to the location of the producer, if not included;

(ii)  for a material purchased in the territory where the good is produced, be the producer's price actually paid or payable for the material including the costs of freight, insurance, packing and all other costs incurred in transporting the material to the location of the producer, if not included; and

(iii) for an intermediate material, be determined by computing the sum of:

   (A) all costs incurred in the production of the material, including general expenses; and

   (B) an amount for profit;

(b) for the value of non-originating materials, the following expenses may be deducted from the value of the material:

(i)   the duties, taxes and customs brokerage fees on the materials paid in the territory of one or more of the Parties, other than the duties and taxes that are waived, refunded, refundable or otherwise recoverable, including credit against duties or taxes paid or payable;

(ii)  inland transportation costs incurred to transport the materials to the local producer;

(iii) the costs of waste and spoilage resulting from the use of the material in the production of the good, less the value of renewable scrap or by-product; and

(iv)  the cost of originating materials used in the production of the non-originating material in the territory of a Party.

## ARTICLE 4.2: ORIGINATING GOODS

1.  For the purposes of this Agreement, an originating good means a good:

   (a) wholly obtained or produced entirely in the territory of one or both of the Parties;

(b) that has satisfied the requirements specified in Annex 4A as well as other applicable requirements under this Chapter as a result of the production occurring entirely in the territory of one or both of the Parties;

(c) otherwise provided as an originating good under this Chapter; or

(d) produced entirely in the territory of one or both of the Parties exclusively from originating materials pursuant to this Chapter.

2. Product-specific rules, requiring that the materials used undergo a change in tariff classification or a specific manufacturing or processing operation, shall apply only to non-originating materials.

### ARTICLE 4.3: TREATMENT OF CERTAIN GOODS

1. The goods listed in Annex 4B shall be originating goods when the goods are imported into the territory of Singapore from the territory of Korea. The goods shall also be originating material for purposes of satisfying the requirements specified in this Chapter.

2. Upon request of a Party, the Parties shall have consultations on the operation or revision of this Article and Annex 4B.

### ARTICLE 4.4: OUTWARD PROCESSING

1. Notwithstanding the relevant provisions of Article 4.2 and the product-specific requirements set out in Annex 4A, a good listed in Annex 4C shall be considered as originating even if it has undergone processes of production or operation outside the territory of a Party on a material exported from the Party and subsequently re-imported to the Party, provided that:

(a) the total value of non-originating inputs as set out in paragraph 2 does not exceed forty (40) per cent of the customs value of the final good for which originating status is claimed;

(b) the value of originating materials is not less than forty-five (45) per cent of the customs value of the final good for which originating status is claimed;

(c) the materials exported from a Party shall have been wholly obtained or produced in the Party or have undergone there processes of production or operation going beyond the non-qualifying operations in Article 4.16, prior to being exported outside the territory of the Party;

(d) the producer of the exported material and the producer of the final good for which originating status is claimed are the same;

(e) the re-imported good has been obtained through the processes of production or operation of the exported material; and

(f)  the last process of production or operation[4-1] takes place in the territory of the Party.

2.   For the purposes of paragraph 1(a), the total value of non-originating inputs shall be the value of any non-originating materials added in a Party as well as the value of any materials added and all other costs accumulated outside the territory of the Party, including transportation cost.

## ARTICLE 4.5: REGIONAL VALUE CONTENT

When a regional value content is required to determine an originating good, the regional value content of a good shall be calculated on the basis of the following method:

$$RVC = \frac{CV - VNM}{CV} \times 100$$

where

RVC      is the regional value content, expressed as a percentage;

CV        is the customs value adjusted to an F.O.B. basis; and

VNM      is the value of non-originating materials used by the producer in the production of the good.

## ARTICLE 4.6: UNASSEMBLED OR DISASSEMBLED GOODS

A good that is imported into the territory of a Party in an unassembled or disassembled form but is classified as an assembled good pursuant to the provisions of sub-paragraph (a) of paragraph 2 of the General Rule for the Interpretation of the Harmonized System shall be considered as an originating good, if the good meets the requirements of Article 4.2.

## ARTICLE 4.7: INTERMEDIATE MATERIALS

Any self-produced material that is used in the production of a good may be designated by the producer of the good as an intermediate material for the purpose of calculating the regional value content of the good under Article 4.5, provided that

---

[4-1] The last process of production or operation does not exclude the non-qualifying operations stipulated in Article 4.16

where the intermediate material is subject to a regional value content requirement, no other self-produced material subject to a regional value content requirement used in the production of that intermediate material may itself be designated by the producer as an intermediate material.

### ARTICLE 4.8: NEUTRAL ELEMENTS

In order to determine whether a good originates it shall not be necessary to determine the origin of the following which might be used in its production and not incorporated into the good:

(a) fuel and energy;
(b) tools, dies and moulds;
(c) spare parts and materials used in the maintenance of equipment and buildings;
(d) lubricants, greases, compounding materials and other materials used in production or used to operate equipment and buildings;
(e) gloves, glasses, footwear, clothing, safety equipment and supplies;
(f) equipment, devices and supplies used for testing or inspecting the goods; and
(g) any other goods that are not incorporated into the good but whose use in the production of the good can reasonably be demonstrated to be a part of that production.

### ARTICLE 4.9: ACCUMULATION

1.   Originating materials from the territory of a Party incorporated in the production of a good in the territory of the other Party, shall be considered to originate in the territory of the other Party.

2.   For the purpose of establishing that a good is originating, the producer of a good may accumulate one's production with the production, in the territory of one or both of the Parties by one or more producers, of materials incorporated in the production of the good, so that the production of those materials is considered as done by that producer, provided that the good complies with the criteria set out in Article 4.2.

### ARTICLE 4.10: DE MINIMIS

1.   A good that does not undergo a change in tariff classification pursuant to Annex 4A shall be considered as originating if:

(a) the value of all non-originating materials used in its production that do not undergo the required change in tariff classification does not exceed ten (10) per cent of the customs value of the good; and

(b) the good meets all other applicable criteria set forth in this Chapter for qualifying as an originating good.

The value of such non-originating materials shall, however, be included in the value of non-originating materials for any applicable regional value content requirement for the good.

2.   Paragraph 1 shall not apply to:

(a) a non-originating material used in the production of a good provided for in Chapters 1 through 14 of the Harmonized System; and

(b) a non-originating material used in the production of a good provided for in Chapters 15 through 24 of the Harmonized System unless the non-originating material is provided for in a different subheading from that of the good for which the origin is being determined under this Article.

3.   A good provided for in Chapters 50 through 63 of the Harmonized System that is not an originating good, because certain fibres or yarns used in the production of the component of the good that determines the tariff classification of the good do not undergo an applicable change in tariff classification set out in Annex 4A, shall nonetheless be considered as originating if the total weight of all such fibres or yarns in that component is not more than eight (8) per cent of the total weight of that component.

### ARTICLE 4.11: FUNGIBLE GOODS AND MATERIALS

1.   The determination of whether fungible goods or materials are originating goods shall be made either by physical segregation of each good or material or through the use of any of the inventory management method, such as averaging, last-in, first-out, or first-in, first-out, recognised in the Generally Accepted Accounting Principles of a Party in which the production is performed or otherwise accepted by the Party in which the production is performed.

2.   Once a particular inventory management method is selected under paragraph 1, that method shall continue to be used for those fungible goods or materials throughout the fiscal year of the person that selected the inventory management method.

**ARTICLE 4.12: ACCESSORIES, SPARE PARTS AND TOOLS**

1.   Accessories, spare parts, or tools, delivered with a good that form part of standard accessories, spare parts or tools of the good, shall be considered as originating if the good is an originating good, and shall be disregarded in determining whether all the non-originating materials used in the production of the good undergo the applicable change in tariff classification set out in Annex 4A, provided that:

    (a)   the accessories, spare parts or tools are not invoiced separately from the good; and

    (b)   the quantities and value of the accessories, spare parts or tools are customary for the good.

2.   If the good is subject to a regional value-content requirement, the value of the accessories, spare parts or tools shall be taken into account as originating or non-originating materials, as the case may be, in calculating the regional value content of the good.

**ARTICLE 4.13: PACKAGING MATERIALS AND CONTAINERS FOR RETAIL SALE**

Packaging materials and containers in which a good is packaged for retail sale shall, if classified with the good, be disregarded in determining whether all the non-originating materials used in the production of the good undergo the applicable change in tariff classification set out in Annex 4A, and, if the good is subject to a regional value content requirement, the value of such packaging materials and containers shall be taken into account as originating or non-originating materials, as the case may be, in calculating the regional value content of the good.

**ARTICLE 4.14: PACKING MATERIALS AND CONTAINERS FOR SHIPMENT**

Packing materials and containers in which a good is packed for shipment shall be disregarded in determining whether:

    (a)   the non-originating materials used in the production of the good undergo an applicable change in tariff classification set out in Annex 4A; and

    (b)   the good satisfies a regional value content requirement.

**ARTICLE 4.15: DIRECT CONSIGNMENT**

A good shall not be considered to be an originating good of a Party by reason of having undergone production that satisfies the requirements of Article 4.2, if, subsequent to that production:

(a) the good is not transported directly to the territory of the other Party; or

(b) where the good is shipped through or transshipped in the territory of a country that is not a Party under this Agreement, the importer has failed to meet the requirements stipulated in paragraph (c) of Article 5.9.

## ARTICLE 4.16: NON-QUALIFYING OPERATIONS

Notwithstanding any provision in this Chapter, a good shall not be considered to have satisfied the requirements for an originating good in Article 4.2 merely by reason of going through certain operations or processes including, *inter alia,* the following:

(a) operations to ensure the preservation of products in good condition during transport and storage (such as drying, freezing, keeping in brine) and other similar operations;

(b) changes of packaging and breaking up and assembly of packages;

(c) affixing marks, labels and other like distinguishing signs on products or their packaging;

(d) disassembly;

(e) testing or calibrations;

(f) placing in bottles, cases, boxes and other simple packaging operations;

(g) simple cutting, including peeling, unshelling or unflaking, grain removing, removal of bones, crushing or squeezing, and macerating;

(h) simple mixing;

(i) simple assembly of parts to constitute a complete product;

(j) simple making-up of sets of articles;

(k) slaughter of animals;

(l) quality check or grinding;

(m) elimination of dust from broken or damaged parts, application of oil, paint for rust treatment or other protecting materials;

(n) salifying or sweetening;

(o) dilution with water or with any other aqueous, ionized or salted solution;

(p) division of bulk shipment; and

(q) a combination of two or more operations referred to in paragraphs (a) through (p),

carried out in the territory of the Parties, when non-originating materials are used in those operations.

**ARTICLE 4.17: INTERPRETATION AND APPLICATION**

For the purposes of this Chapter:

(a)  the basis for tariff classification in this Chapter is the Harmonised System as amended on January 1, 2002;

(b)  in applying the Customs Valuation Agreement for the determination of the origin of a good under this Chapter:

(i)  the principles of the Customs Valuation Agreement shall apply to domestic transactions, with such modifications as may be required by the circumstances, as would apply to international transactions;

(ii)  the provisions of this Chapter shall take precedence over the Customs Valuation Agreement to the extent of any difference; and

(iii) the definitions in Article 4.1 shall take precedence over the definitions in the Customs Valuation Agreement to the extent of any difference; and

(c)  all costs referred to in this Chapter shall be recorded and maintained in accordance with the Generally Accepted Accounting Principles applicable in the territory of the Party in which the good is produced.

**ARTICLE 4.18: CONSULTATIONS AND MODIFICATIONS**

1.   The Parties shall consult and co-operate to ensure that this Chapter is applied in an effective and uniform manner.

2.   The Parties shall consult to review the rules of origin and discuss necessary amendments to this Chapter and its Annexes, as provided in Article 22.1 or upon the request of a Party, taking into account developments in technology, production processes, and other related matters including the recommended amendments to the Harmonized System.

## CHAPTER 5
## CUSTOMS PROCEDURES

ARTICLE 5.1: DEFINITIONS

For the purposes of this Chapter:

**certificate of origin** means respective forms used for purposes of claiming preferential tariff treatment in the importing Party, certifying that an exported good qualifies as an originating good in accordance with Chapter 4 (Rules of Origin), on the basis of documentary evidence or reliable information;

**certification body** means a body referred to in Annex 5A;

**customs administration** means the competent authority that is responsible under the law of a Party for the administration of customs laws and regulations;

**exporter** means a person located in the territory of a Party from where a good is exported by such a person;

**importer** means a person located in the territory of a Party where a good is imported by such a person;

**identical goods** means "identical goods" as defined in the Customs Valuation Agreement;

**producer** is as defined in Article 4.1;

**production** is as defined in Article 4.1;

**Cost and Production Statement** means a declaration made by the producer, in the calculation of the regional value content, the HS tariff classifications of the product and its non-originating material used, to determine the originating status of the good. The declaration should be signed by a designated authority, generally the managing director or accountant of the company. The declaration may be made by the importer or exporter, if he or she has pertinent information to the production of the good. Notwithstanding the above, the producer shall not be required to provide the information to the importer or the exporter;

**value** means value of a good or material for purposes of calculating customs duties or for purposes of applying Chapter 4 (Rules of Origin);

**Declaration for Preference** means an application for claiming preferential tariff treatment declared, on the basis of a certificate of origin or any other documentary evidence of origin, by an importer to the customs administration as part of the import application that an imported good qualifies as an originating good in accordance with Chapter 4.

ARTICLE **5.2:** CERTIFICATE OF ORIGIN

1.   The Parties shall adopt two respective forms of the certificate of origin as set out in Annex 5B and Annex 5C, which may be revised by agreement between the Parties.

2.   The respective certificate of origin, referred to in paragraph 1, shall be issued by the certification bodies of the exporting Party.

3.   The issued certificate of origin shall be valid for twelve (12) months from the date of issue.

4.   Each Party shall inform, through its customs administration, the other Party of the names and addresses of the authorised signatories issuing this certificate of origin and shall provide specimen impressions of signatures and official seals used by such signatories. Any change in names, addresses, signatures or official seals shall be promptly notified to the other Party.

5.   Each Party shall:

   (a)   require an exporter in its territory to complete and sign an application for certificate of origin for any good which an importer may claim preferential tariff treatment on importation of the good into the territory of the other Party; and
   (b)   provide that where an exporter in its territory is not the producer of the good, the exporter may complete and sign an application for a certificate of origin on the basis of:
      (i)   the exporter's knowledge that the good qualifies as an originating good; or
      (ii)   the exporter's reasonable reliance on the producer's written representation that the good qualifies as an originating good.

6.   The certificate of origin shall be issued in the English language.

7.   Each Party shall provide that a certificate of origin that has been issued by authorised body designated by each Party is applicable to a single importation of a good into its territory.

8.   In cases where a certificate of origin has not been issued at the time of exportation or soon thereafter due to involuntary errors or omissions or other valid causes, the certificate of origin may be issued retrospectively but not later than one year from the date of shipment.

### ARTICLE 5.3: CLAIMS FOR PREFERENTIAL TREATMENT

1.   Each Party shall require an importer in its territory that claims preferential tariff treatment for a good imported into its territory from the territory of the other Party to:

   (a)   make a declaration for preference as part of the import application prescribed by its legislation, based on importer's knowledge or information including a valid certificate of origin, that the good qualifies as an originating good;
   (b)   submit the certificate of origin or other documentary evidence of origin at the time of the declaration referred to in subparagraph (a), to its customs administration upon request; and
   (c)   promptly make a corrected declaration and pay any duties owing, where the importer has reason to believe that a certificate of origin on which a declaration was based contains information that is incorrect.

2.   Each Party shall provide that the importing Party applies preferential tariff treatment only in cases where an importer proves the accuracy of origin of the imported goods through documentary evidence or any other relevant information in accordance with its laws and regulations.

3.   A Party may deny preferential tariff treatment to an imported good if the importer fails to comply with requirements of this Chapter.

4.   The importing Party shall grant preferential tariff treatment to goods imported after the date of entry into force of this Agreement, in cases where the importer does not have the certificate of origin or other documentary evidence of origin at the time of importation, provided that:

   (a)   the importer had, at the time of importation, indicated to the customs administration of the importing Party his intention to claim preferential tariff treatment; and
   (b)   the certificate of origin or other documentary evidence of origin is submitted to its customs administration within such period from the date of payment of customs duties in accordance with the domestic laws and regulations in the importing Party.

## ARTICLE 5.4: OBLIGATIONS RELATING TO EXPORTATIONS

1.  Each Party shall provide that an exporter or a producer in its territory shall submit a copy of the certificate of origin or other documentary evidence of origin to its customs administration upon request.

2.  Each Party shall provide that a false statement by an exporter or a producer in its territory that a good to be exported to the territory of the other Party qualifies as an originating good shall be penalised for a contravention of its customs laws and regulations regarding the making of a false statement or representation. Furthermore, each Party may apply such measures as the circumstances may warrant where an exporter or a producer in its territory fails to comply with any requirement of this Chapter.

### ARTICLE 5.5: RECORD KEEPING REQUIREMENT

1.  Each Party shall provide that an exporter and a producer in its territory that has obtained a certificate of origin shall maintain in its territory, for five (5) years after the date on which the certificate of origin was issued or for such longer period as the Party may specify, all records relating to the origin of a good for which preferential tariff treatment was claimed in the territory of the other Party, including records associated with:

    (a) the purchase of, cost of, value of, shipping of, and payment for, the good that is exported from its territory;

    (b) the sourcing of, the purchase of, cost of, value of, and payment for, all materials, including neutral elements, used in the production of the good that is exported from its territory; and

    (c) the production of the good in the form in which the good is exported from its territory.

2.  Each Party shall provide that an importer claiming preferential tariff treatment for a good imported into the Party's territory shall maintain in that territory, for five (5) years after the date of importation of the good or for such longer period as the Party may specify, such documentation, including a copy of the certificate of origin, as the Party may require relating to the importation of the good.

3.  The records to be maintained in accordance with paragraphs 1 and 2 shall include electronic records and shall be maintained in accordance with the domestic laws and practices of each Party.

### ARTICLE 5.6: WAIVER OF CERTIFICATE OF ORIGIN

1.   Notwithstanding paragraph 1(b) of Article 5.3, a certificate of origin shall not be required for:

(a)   an importation of a good whose aggregate customs value does not exceed USD 1,000 or its equivalent amount in the Party's currency, or such higher amount as it may establish; or

(b)   an importation of a good into the territory of the importing Party, for which the importing Party has waived the requirement for a certificate of origin in accordance with its domestic laws and practices;

provided that the importation does not form part of one or more importations that may reasonably be considered to have been undertaken or arranged for the purpose of avoiding the certification requirements of Articles 5.2 and 5.3.

2.   The importing Party may request the importer in paragraph 1 to provide relevant documents to certify that the good qualifies as an originating good.

### ARTICLE 5.7: VERIFICATIONS FOR PREFERENTIAL TARIFF TREATMENT

1.   For the purposes of determining whether a good imported into its territory from the territory of the other Party is eligible for preferential tariff treatment, the importing Party may, through its customs administration, conduct a verification, which may be in sequence, by means of:

(a)   request for a certificate of origin from the importer;

(b)   request for Cost and Production Statement and information from the importer for cases where the importer is able to prepare it on the basis of the importer's own documentary evidence or information;

(c)   request for Cost and Production Statement and information from an exporter or a producer in the territory of the other Party through the other Party's customs administration;

(d)   visit to the premises of an exporter or a producer in the territory of the other Party to review the records referred to in paragraph 1 of Article 5.5 and observe the facilities used in the production of the good, or to that effect any facilities used in the production of the materials; or

(e)   such other procedure as the Parties may agree to.

2.   The importer, exporter or producer that receives a written request pursuant to subparagraphs (a), (b) or (c) of paragraph 1 shall answer and return it within a period of thirty (30) days from the date on which it was received. During this period, the importer, exporter or producer may have one opportunity to make a

written request to the Party conducting the verification for an extension of the answering period, for a period not exceeding thirty (30) days.

3. In the case where the importer, exporter, or producer does not return the written request for information made by the importing Party within the given period or its extension, or that the information provided is false or incomplete, the Party may deny preferential tariff treatment.

4. Prior to conducting a verification visit pursuant to subparagraph 1(d), a Party shall, through its customs administration:

    (a) deliver a written notification of its intention to conduct the visit to:
        (i) the exporter or producer whose premises are to be visited; and
        (ii) the customs administration of the other Party; and
    (b) obtain the written consent of the exporter or producer whose premises are to be visited.

5. Where an exporter or producer has not given its written consent to a proposed verification visit within thirty (30) days from the receipt of notification pursuant to paragraph 4, the notifying Party may deny preferential tariff treatment to the relevant good.

6. Each Party shall provide that, upon receipt of notification pursuant to paragraph 4, such an exporter or producer may, within fifteen (15) days of receiving the notification, have one opportunity to request to the Party conducting the verification for a postponement of the proposed verification visit, for a period not exceeding sixty (60) days. This extension shall be notified to the customs administration of the importing and exporting Parties.

7. A Party shall not deny preferential tariff treatment to a good solely because a verification visit was postponed pursuant to paragraph 6.

8. After the conclusion of a verification visit, the Party conducting the verification, shall provide the exporter or producer whose good was verified, with a written determination of whether the good is eligible for preferential tariff treatment, based on the relevant law and findings of fact.

9. Where verifications by a Party show that an exporter or producer repeatedly makes false or unsupported representations that a good imported into the Party's territory qualifies as an originating good, the Party may suspend the preferential tariff treatment to be accorded to subsequent shipment of identical good exported or produced by such a person until that person establishes that the shipment complies with Chapter 4 (Rules of Origin), in accordance with its domestic laws, regulations

or practices. The importing Party shall inform the customs administration of the exporting Party on the evidence and details of the suspension made.

### ARTICLE 5.8: ADVANCE RULINGS

1.   Prior to the importation of a good into its territory, each Party, through its customs administration, shall provide for the issuance of written advance rulings to an importer of the good in its territory or to an exporter or producer of the good in the other Party's territory concerning tariff classification, questions arising from the application of the Customs Valuation Agreement and country of origin so as to determine whether the good qualifies as an originating good.

2.   Each Party shall adopt or maintain procedures for the issuance of advance rulings, including:

   (a)   the provision that an importer or its agent in its territory or an exporter or producer or their agent in the territory of the other Party may request such a ruling prior to the importation in question;
   (b)   a detailed description of the information required to process a request for an advance ruling; and
   (c)   the provision that the advance ruling be based on the facts and circumstances presented by the person requesting the ruling.

3.   Each Party shall provide that its customs administrations:

   (a)   may request, at any time during the course of evaluating an application for an advance ruling, additional information necessary to evaluate the application;
   (b)   shall issue the advance ruling expeditiously, and in any case within ninety (90) days of obtaining all necessary information; and
   (c)   shall provide, upon request of the person who requested the advance ruling, a full explanation of the reasons for the ruling.

4.   The importing Party may modify or revoke the issued ruling:

   (a)   if the ruling was based on an error of fact;
   (b)   if there is a change in the material facts or circumstances on which the ruling was based;
   (c)   to conform with an amendment to this Agreement; or
   (d)   to conform with a judicial or administration decision or a change in its domestic laws and regulations.

5.   Each Party shall provide that any modification or revocation of an advance ruling is effective on the date on which the modification or revocation is issued, or on such a later date as may be specified therein, and shall not be applied to importations of a good that have occurred prior to that date, unless the person to whom the advance ruling was issued has not acted in accordance with its terms and conditions.

6.   Notwithstanding paragraph 5, the issuing Party shall postpone the effective date of such modification or revocation for a period not exceeding sixty (60) days where the person to whom the advance ruling was issued demonstrates that it has relied in good faith to its detriment on that ruling.

7.   Each Party shall provide that where it issues an advance ruling to a person that has misrepresented or omitted material facts or circumstances or failed to act in accordance with the terms and conditions of the ruling, the Party may impose penalties or deny the preferential tariff treatment as the circumstances may warrant.

8.   A good that is subject to an origin verification process or any instance of review or appeal in the territory of one of the Parties may not be the subject of an advance ruling.

9.   Subject to paragraph 10, each Party shall apply an advance ruling to importations into its territory of the relevant good from the date of its issuance or from such later date as may be specified in the ruling.

10.   The importing Party shall apply the advance ruling for three (3) years from the date of issuance of the ruling.

### ARTICLE 5.9: DENIAL OF PREFERENTIAL TARIFF TREATMENT

Except as otherwise provided in this Chapter, each Party may, notwithstanding the requirements of Articles 5.3, 5.4, 5.5, 5.6 and 5.7 and any other legal requirements imposed under its law have been satisfied, deny the applicable preferential tariff treatment to an originating good imported into its territory:

(a)   if the declared origin of the imported good is not supported by documentary evidence presented by an importer in its territory, or an exporter or a producer in the territory of the other Party;

(b)   if an exporter or a producer in the territory of the other Party does not allow the customs administration of the importing Party access to information required to make a determination of whether the goods or the materials is originating by the following or other means:

    (i)   denial of access to its records and/or documents;

    (ii)  failure to respond to a cost and production statement or information requested; or

    (iii) failure to maintain records or documentation relevant to determine the origin of the good in accordance with the requirement of this Chapter;

(c)  if, where the good is shipped through or transshipped in the territory of a country that is not a Party under this Agreement, the importer of the good does not provide, on the request of that Party's customs administration:

    (i)   a copy of the customs control documents that indicate, to the satisfaction of the importing Party's customs administration, that the goods remained under customs control while in the territory of such non-Parties;

    (ii)  any other information given by the customs administration of such non-Parties or other relevant entities, which evidences that they have not undergone, in such non-Parties, operation other than unloading, reloading, crating, packing, repacking or any other operation necessary to keep them in good condition; or

    (iii) any other information or commercial documents given by the importer which evidence that they have not undergone, in such non-Parties, operation other than unloading, reloading, crating, packing, repacking or any other operation necessary to keep them in good condition; or

(d)  if, within thirty (30) days after the request of the customs administration of the importing Party, the producer, exporter or importer of a good, which has undergone processes of production or operation outside the territory of a Party, fails to submit all the necessary documentary evidence to prove that the good satisfies all the requirements set out in Article 4.4, including that has been obtained from the performer of the processes of production or operation outside the territory of the Party. Notwithstanding the above, the producer, exporter or importer of a good may have one opportunity to make a written request to the customs administration of the importing Party for an extension of the submission period, for a period not exceeding thirty (30) days.

## ARTICLE 5.10: TEMPORARY ADMISSION AND GOODS IN TRANSIT

1.   Each Party shall continue to facilitate the procedures for the temporary admission of goods traded between the Parties in accordance with the Customs Convention on the A.T.A. Carnet for the Temporary Admission of Goods.

2.   Each Party shall continue to facilitate customs clearance of goods in transit from or to the territory of the other Party.

**ARTICLE 5.11: REVIEW AND APPEAL**

1.  Each Party shall grant substantially the same rights of review and appeal of determinations of origin and advance rulings by its customs administration, as it provides to importers in its territory, to any person:

(a)  who has obtained a certificate of origin or completed a cost and production statement for a good that has been the subject of a determination of origin under this Chapter; or

(b)  who has received an advance ruling pursuant to Article 5.8.

2.  Each Party shall provide that the rights of review and appeal referred to in paragraph 1 shall include access to:

(a)  at least one level of administrative review[5-1] independent of the official or office responsible for the determination under review; and

(b)  in accordance with its domestic law, judicial or quasi-judicial review of the determination or decision taken at the final level of administrative review[5-2].

**ARTICLE 5.12: PENALTIES**

Each Party shall maintain measures imposing criminal or administrative penalties, whether solely or in combination, for violations of its laws and regulations relating to this Chapter.

**ARTICLE 5.13: CUSTOMS CO-OPERATION**

The Parties shall co-operate through their respective customs administrations on:

(a)  Verification of Origin:
    (i)  The Parties shall co-operate through their respective customs administrations in the origin verification process of a good, for which the customs administration of the importing Party may request the other Party's customs administrations to co-operate in this process of verification in its own territory; and

---

[5-1] For Singapore, the level of administrative review may include the Ministry supervising the Customs administration.

[5-2] The review of the determination or decision taken at the final level of administrative review inG Singapore may take the form of a common law judicial review.

    (ii)   A Party may, if it considers necessary, station customs liaison officers in the local embassy to work with the host government, for information exchange pertaining to origin verification;

(b)  Paperless Customs Clearance:

    (i)   The Parties shall, as they deem fit, simplify and streamline customs procedures through the domestic integration of customs systems with other controlling agencies, with a view to enhancing paperless customs clearance;

    (ii)   The Parties shall endeavour to provide an electronic environment that supports business transactions between their respective customs administrations and their trading communities; and

    (iii)   The Parties shall exchange views and information on realising and promoting paperless customs clearance between their respective customs administrations and their trading communities;

(c)  Risk Management:

    (i)   The Parties shall adopt risk management approach in its customs activities based on its identified risk of goods in order to facilitate the clearance of low risk consignments, while focusing its inspection activities on high-risk goods; and

    (ii)   The Parties shall exchange information on risk management techniques in the performance of their customs procedures;

(d)  Sharing of Best Practices and Information:

    (i)   The Parties may, as they deem fit, organise training programmes in customs-related issues, which should include training for customs officials as well as users that directly participate in customs procedures; and

    (ii)   The Parties may, as they deem fit, facilitate initiatives for the exchange of information on best practices in relation to customs procedures and matters in accordance with their respective domestic customs laws; and

(e)  Transparency:

    (i)   Each Party shall ensure that its laws, regulations, guidelines, procedures, and administrative rulings governing customs matters are promptly published, either on the Internet or in print form;

    (ii)   Each Party shall designate, establish, and maintain one or more inquiry points to address inquiries from interested persons pertaining to customs matters, and shall make available on the Internet information concerning procedures for making such inquiries; and

    (iii)   For the purposes of certainty, nothing in this Article or in any part of this Agreement shall require any Party to publish law enforcement procedures and internal operational guidelines including those related to conducting risk analysis and targeting methodologies.

**ARTICLE 5.14: IMPLEMENTATION OF OBLIGATIONS**

1. The provisions in this Chapter must be implemented by the Parties by the time that this Agreement enters into force.

2. Each Party must implement all its obligations through the institution of legal or administrative changes and where necessary amend its domestic laws to support the implementation of the obligations undertaken.

**ARTICLE 5.15: CUSTOMS CONTACT POINTS AND AD HOC CUSTOMS COMMITTEE**

1. Each Party shall discharge all its obligations that are undertaken in accordance with this Chapter.

2. Each Party shall designate the contact point set out in Annex 5D for all matters relating to this Chapter and Chapter 4 (Rules of Origin).

3. Upon the receipt of any matter raised by the customs administration of a Party, the customs administration of the other Party shall assign its own experts to look into the matter and to respond with its findings and proposed solution for resolving the matter within a reasonable time.

4. The Parties shall endeavour to resolve any matter raised under this Article through consultations between contact points. If the matter cannot be so resolved, the matter shall be referred to a customs committee established on an ad hoc basis pursuant to Article 22.1.

**ARTICLE 5.16: CONFIDENTIALITY**

1. Nothing in this Agreement shall be construed to require a Party to furnish or allow access to confidential information, the disclosure of which would impede law enforcement, be contrary to the public interest, or prejudice the legitimate commercial interests of particular enterprises, public or private.

2. Each Party shall, in accordance with its domestic laws, maintain the confidentiality of information collected pursuant to this Chapter and protect it from disclosure that could prejudice the competitive position of the persons providing the information.

**ARTICLE 5.17: REVIEW**

The Parties shall review the certification system agreed under this Chapter for issuing the certificate of origin at the review as provided in Article 22.1.

## CHAPTER 6
## TRADE REMEDIES

### ARTICLE 6.1: DEFINITIONS

For the purposes of this Chapter:

**domestic industry** means the producers as a whole of the like or directly competitive products operating within the territory of a Party, or those whose collective output of the like or directly competitive products constitute a major proportion of the total domestic production of those products;

**global safeguard measure** means a measure applied under Article XIX of GATT 1994 and the WTO Agreement on Safeguards;

**serious injury** means a significant overall impairment in the position of a domestic industry;

**substantial cause** means a cause which is important and not less than any other cause; and

**threat of serious injury** means serious injury that, on the basis of facts and not merely on allegation, conjecture or remote possibility, is clearly imminent.

### ARTICLE 6.2: ANTI-DUMPING MEASURES

1.   The Parties maintain their rights and obligations under Article VI of GATT 1994 and the Agreement on Implementation of Article VI of GATT 1994 ("WTO Agreement on Anti-dumping").

2.   Anti-dumping actions taken pursuant to Articles VI of GATT 1994 and the WTO Agreement on Anti-dumping shall not be subject to Chapter 20 (Dispute Settlement).

3.   Notwithstanding paragraph 1, the Parties shall observe the following practices in anti-dumping cases between them in order to enhance transparency in the implementation of the WTO Anti-dumping Agreement:

   (a)   when anti-dumping margins are established on the weighted average basis, all individual margins, whether positive or negative, should be counted toward the average; and

(b) if a decision is taken to impose an anti-dumping duty pursuant to Article 9.1 of the WTO Agreement on Anti-dumping, the Party taking such a decision, should apply the "lesser duty" rule, by imposing a duty which is less than the dumping margin where such lesser duty would be adequate to remove the injury to the domestic industry.

### ARTICLE 6.3: COUNTERVAILING MEASURES

1. The Parties maintain their rights and obligations under Article VI of GATT 1994 and the WTO Agreement on Subsidies and Countervailing Measures.

2. Countervailing measures taken pursuant to Article VI of GATT 1994 and the WTO Agreement on Subsidies and Countervailing Measures shall not be subject to Chapter 20 (Dispute Settlement).

### ARTICLE 6.4: BILATERAL SAFEGUARD MEASURES

1. Subject to paragraphs 2, 3, 4, 5, 6, 7 and 8, if, as a result of the reduction or elimination of a customs duty under this Agreement, an originating good of the other Party is being imported into the territory of a Party in such increased quantities, in absolute terms or relative to domestic production, and under such conditions that the imports of such originating good from the other Party constitute a substantial cause of serious injury or threat thereof, to a domestic industry producing a like or directly competitive good, such Party may:

(a) suspend further reduction of any rate of customs duty provided for under this Agreement for such originating good; or
(b) increase the rate of customs duty on such originating good to a level not to exceed the lesser of:
  (i) the most-favoured-nation ("MFN") applied rate of duty on the good in effect at the time the action is taken; and
  (ii) the MFN applied rate of duty on the good in effect on the day immediately preceding the date of entry into force of this Agreement.

2. A Party shall take a measure only following an investigation by that Party's competent authorities in accordance with Article 3 and paragraph 2 of Article 4 of the WTO Agreement on Safeguards. To this end, Article 3 and paragraph 2 of Article 4 of the WTO Agreement on Safeguards are incorporated into and made a part of this Agreement, *mutatis mutandis*. The investigation shall in all cases be completed within one year following its date of initiation.

3.   A Party shall notify the other Party in writing upon initiation of an investigation provided for in paragraph 2 and shall consult with the other Party as far in advance of taking any such measure as practicable, with a view to reviewing the information arising from the investigation, exchanging views on the measure and reaching an agreement on compensation as set out in paragraph 8. If a Party takes a provisional measure pursuant to paragraph 7, the Party shall also notify the other Party prior to taking such measure, and shall initiate consultations with the other Party immediately after such measure is taken.

4.   No measure may be maintained:

(a)  except to the extent and for such period of time as may be necessary to prevent or remedy serious injury and to facilitate adjustment; or

(b)  for a period exceeding two (2) years; except that the period may be extended by up to two (2) years if the competent authorities determine, in conformity with the procedures set out in paragraphs 1 through 3, that the measure continues to be necessary to prevent or remedy serious injury and to facilitate adjustment and that there is evidence that the industry is adjusting.

5.   Where the expected duration of the measure is over one year, the Party applying such measure shall progressively liberalise it at regular intervals during the period of application.

6.   Upon the termination of the measure, the rate of customs duty shall be the rate which would have been in effect but for the measure.

7.   In critical circumstances, where delay would cause damage which would be difficult to repair, a Party may take a measure described in paragraph 1 on a provisional basis pursuant to a preliminary determination that there is clear evidence that imports from the other Party have increased as the result of the reduction or elimination of a customs duty under this Agreement, and such imports constitute a substantial cause of serious injury, or threat thereof, to the domestic industry. The duration of such provisional measure shall not exceed 200 days, during which time the requirements of paragraph 2 shall be met. Any tariff increases shall be promptly refunded if the investigation provided for in paragraph 2 does not result in a finding that the requirements of paragraph 1 are met. The duration of any provisional measure shall be counted as part of the period described in paragraph 4.

8.   The Party applying a measure described in paragraph 1 shall provide to the other Party mutually agreed trade liberalising compensation in the form of concessions having substantially equivalent trade effects or equivalent to the value of the additional duties expected to result from the measure. If the Parties are

unable to agree on compensation within thirty (30) days in the consultations under paragraph 3, the Party against whose originating good the measure is applied may take action with respect to originating goods of the other Party that has trade effects substantially equivalent to the measure. The Party taking such action shall apply the action only for the minimum period necessary to achieve the substantially equivalent effects, and in any event, only while the measure under paragraph 1 is being applied.

### ARTICLE 6.5: GLOBAL SAFEGUARD MEASURES

1.   The Parties maintain their rights and obligations under Article XIX of GATT 1994 and the WTO Agreement on Safeguards.

2.   Actions taken pursuant to paragraph 1 of this Article shall not be subject to Chapter 20 (Dispute Settlement).

## CHAPTER 7
## SANITARY AND PHYTOSANITARY MEASURES

### ARTICLE 7.1: SANITARY AND PHYTOSANITARY MEASURES

1.   The Parties shall not apply their sanitary and phytosanitary measures in a manner which would constitute a means of arbitrary or unjustifiable discrimination or a disguised restriction on international trade.

2.   The Parties shall ensure that any sanitary and phytosanitary measure is applied only to the extent necessary to protect human, animal or plant life or health, is based on scientific principles and is not maintained without sufficient scientific evidence.

3.   The principles set out in paragraphs 1 and 2 shall be applied in accordance with the WTO Agreement on the Application of Sanitary and Phytosanitary Measures which is hereby incorporated into and made part of this Agreement.

4.   To provide a means of consultation and exchange of information between the Parties on sanitary and phytosanitary matters and enable the response to queries from one Party to the other within a reasonable time, the Parties shall maintain and communicate through the following contact points[7-1]:

   (a)   for Korea, the Ministry of Agriculture and Forestry; and
   (b)   for Singapore, Agri-Food and Veterinary Authority.

---

[7-1] The communications and essential information exchanged between the Parties shall be in the English language. Particulars relating to the contact points shall be exchanged at the earliest possible, after the entry into force of this Agreement. The Parties understand that the communications between the Parties can be made via fax, e-mail or any other means agreed to by the Parties.

## CHAPTER 8
## TECHNICAL BARRIERS TO TRADE AND MUTUAL RECOGNITION

ARTICLE 8.1: OBJECTIVE

The objectives of this Chapter are to increase and facilitate trade between the Parties through:

(a) the full implementation of the WTO Agreement on Technical Barriers to Trade ( "WTO TBT Agreement");
(b) enhancing bilateral co-operation by deepening their mutual understanding and awareness of their respective standards, technical regulations and conformity assessment systems; and
(c) creating and improving the business climate so as to increase business opportunities.

ARTICLE 8.2: SCOPE AND MODALITIES

1. This Chapter applies to standards, technical regulations and conformity assessment procedures that may directly or indirectly affect trade in goods between the Parties and/or assessments of manufacturers or manufacturing processes.

2. The Parties shall intensify their joint work in the field of standards, technical regulations, and conformity assessment procedures and/or assessments of manufacturers or manufacturing processes, with a view to facilitating market access. In particular, the Parties shall seek to identify initiatives that are appropriate for particular issues or sectors. Such initiatives may include co-operation on regulatory issues, such as, alignment to international standards, reliance on supplier's declaration of conformity, and use of accreditations to qualify conformity assessment bodies.

3. In this respect, the Parties recognise that a broad range of mechanisms exists to facilitate the acceptance of conformity assessment results, including:

(a) agreements on mutual acceptance of the results of conformity assessment procedures with respect to specified regulations conducted by bodies located in the territory of the other Party;
(b) accreditation procedures for qualifying conformity assessment bodies;
(c) government designation of conformity assessment bodies;
(d) recognition by a Party of the results of conformity assessments performed in the other Party's territory;
(e) voluntary arrangements between conformity assessment bodies from each Party's territory; and

(f) the importing Party's acceptance of a supplier's declaration of conformity.

To this end, the Parties shall intensify their exchanges of information on the variety of mechanisms to facilitate the acceptance of conformity assessment results. Any such arrangements shall be formalised in a Sectoral Annex, as appropriate.

4.   In accordance with Article 2.4 of the WTO TBT Agreement, where technical regulations are required and relevant international standards exist or their completion is imminent, the Parties shall use them, or the relevant parts of such standards, as a basis for their Mandatory Requirements, except when such international standards or relevant parts of such standards would be an ineffective or inappropriate means for the legitimate objectives pursued, for instance, as a result of fundamental climatic or geographical factors or fundamental technological problems.

5.   In determining whether an international standard, guide, or recommendation within the meaning of Articles 2 and 5, and Annex 3 of the WTO TBT Agreement exists, each Party shall apply the principles set out in "Section IX (Decision of the Committee on Principles for the Development of International Standards, Guides and Recommendations with relation to Articles 2 and 5, and Annex 3 of the Agreement) in the Decisions and Recommendations adopted by the Committee since 1 January 1995", G/TBT/1/Rev.8, 23 May 2002 and its Revision issued by the WTO Committee on Technical Barriers to Trade.

6.   This Chapter does not apply to sanitary and phytosanitary measures as defined in the WTO Agreement on Application of Sanitary and Phytosanitary Measures which are covered by Chapter 7 (Sanitary and Phytosanitary Measures).

ARTICLE 8.3: DEFINITIONS

1.   For the purposes of this Chapter, all general terms concerning standards, and conformity assessment used in this Chapter shall have the meaning given in the definitions contained in the International Organisation for Standardisation/International Electrotechnical Commission (ISO/IEC) Guide 2:2004 "Standardization and related activities – General vocabulary" and ISO/IEC 17000:2004 "Conformity assessment – Vocabulary and general principles" published by the ISO and IEC, unless the context otherwise requires and as appropriate.

2.   In addition, the following terms and definitions shall apply to this Chapter and its Sectoral Annexes unless a more specific meaning is given in the specified Sectoral Annex:

**accept** means the use of the results of conformity assessment procedures as a basis for regulatory actions such as approvals, licences, registrations and post-market assessments of conformity assessment;

**acceptance** has an equivalent meaning to **accept**;

**certification body** means a body, including product or quality systems certification bodies, that may be designated by a Party in accordance with this Chapter to conduct certification on compliance with its or the other Party's standards and/or specifications to meet relevant mandatory requirements;

**confirmation** means the confirmation of the compliance of the manufacturing or test facility with the criteria for confirmation by a competent authority of a Party pursuant to the mandatory requirements of the other Party;

**competent authority** means an authority of a Party with the power to conduct inspection or audits on facilities in its territory to confirm their compliance with mandatory requirements;

**conformity assessment** means any procedure concerned with determining directly or indirectly whether products, manufacturers or manufacturing processes fulfil relevant standards and/or specifications to meet relevant mandatory requirements set out in the respective Party's mandatory requirements. The typical examples of conformity assessment procedures are sampling, testing, inspection, evaluation, verification, certification, registration, accreditation and approval, or their combinations;

**conformity assessment body ("CAB")** means a body that conducts conformity assessment procedures;

**designation** means the authorisation by a Party's designating authority of its CAB to undertake specified conformity assessment procedures pursuant to the mandatory requirements of the other Party;

**designate** has an equivalent meaning to "designation";

**Designating Authority** means a body established in the territory of a Party with the authority to designate, monitor, suspend or withdraw designation of conformity assessment bodies to conduct conformity assessment procedures within its jurisdiction in accordance with the other Party's mandatory requirements;

**mandatory requirements** means a Party's applicable laws, regulations and administrative provisions;

mutual recognition means that each Party, on the basis that it is accorded reciprocal treatment by the other Party:

(a) accepts the test reports of conformity assessment procedures of the other Party to demonstrate conformity of products and/or manufacturers/ manufacturing processes with its mandatory requirements when the conformity assessment procedures are undertaken by conformity assessment bodies designated by the other Party in accordance with this Chapter, i.e., mutual recognition of test reports; or

(b) accepts the certification of results of conformity assessment procedures of the other Party to demonstrate conformity of products and/or manufacturers/manufacturing processes with its mandatory requirements when the conformity assessment procedures are undertaken by conformity assessment bodies designated by the other Party in accordance with this Chapter, i.e., mutual recognition of certification of conformity assessment;

**registered conformity assessment body ("registered CAB")** means a CAB registered pursuant to Article 8.5;

**registration** means the authorisation by a Party's Designating Authority of a CAB proposed by the other Party to undertake specified conformity assessment procedures pursuant to the Party's mandatory requirements;

**Regulatory Authority** means an entity that exercises a legal right to determine the mandatory requirements, control the import, use or supply of products within a Party's territory and may take enforcement action to ensure that products marketed within its territory comply with that Party's mandatory requirements including assessments of manufacturers/manufacturing processes of products;

**Sectoral Annex** is an Annex to this Chapter which specifies the implementation arrangements in respect of a specific product sector;

**stipulated requirements** means the criteria set out in a Sectoral Annex for the designation of CAB;

**technical regulations** shall have the same meaning as in the WTO TBT Agreement;

**test facility** means a facility, including independent laboratories, manufacturers' own test facilities or government testing bodies, that may be designated by one Party's Designating Authority in accordance with this Chapter to undertake tests according to the other Party's mandatory requirements; and

**verification** means an action to verify in the territories of the Parties, by such means as audits or inspections, compliance with the stipulated requirements for designation or criteria for confirmation by a conformity assessment body or a manufacturing or test facility respectively.

3.    For the purposes of this Chapter the singular should be read to include the plural and vice-versa, when appropriate.

ARTICLE 8.4: ORIGIN

This Chapter applies to all products and/or assessments of manufacturers or manufacturing processes of products traded between the Parties, regardless of the origin of those products, unless otherwise specified in a Sectoral Annex, or unless otherwise specified by any mandatory requirement of a Party.

ARTICLE 8.5: MUTUAL RECOGNITION OF CONFORMITY ASSESSMENT

*Scope*

1.    This Article shall apply to:

   (a) mandatory requirements and/or assessments of manufacturers or manufacturing processes, maintained by the Parties to fulfill their legitimate objectives and appropriate level of protection; and
   (b) the conformity assessment bodies and conformity assessment procedures for products as may be specified in the Sectoral Annexes.

2.    For the purposes of this Article, a Sectoral Annex shall include *inter alia*:

   (a) provisions on scope and coverage;
   (b) applicable laws, regulations and administrative provisions, i.e., mandatory requirements of each Party concerning the scope and coverage;
   (c) applicable laws, regulations and administrative provisions of each Party stipulating the requirements covered by this Article, all the conformity

assessment procedures covered by this Article to satisfy such requirements and the stipulated requirements or criteria for designation of conformity assessment bodies or the confirmation of the manufacturing or test facilities covered by this Article; and

(d) the list of Designating Authorities or competent authorities.

## Obligations

3.    Each Party shall accept, in accordance with the provisions of this Article, the results of conformity assessment procedures required by the mandatory requirements of that Party specified in the relevant Sectoral Annex, including certificates and marks of conformity, that are conducted by the registered CABs of the other Party.

4.    Korea shall accept the results of conformity assessment procedures to demonstrate conformity of products with its mandatory requirements when the conformity assessment procedures are undertaken by CABs designated by Singapore's Designating Authority and registered by Korea's Designating Authority in accordance with this Article.

5.    Singapore shall accept the results of conformity assessment procedures to demonstrate conformity of products with its mandatory requirements when the conformity assessment procedures are undertaken by CABs designated by Korea's Designating Authority and registered by Singapore's Designating Authority in accordance with this Article.

## Designating Authorities

6.    For the purposes of this Article, each Party shall:

(a) unless otherwise provided in the relevant Sectoral Annex, designate a single Designating Authority to designate CABs to conduct conformity assessment procedures for products traded between the Parties, whether imports or exports;

(b) then notify the other Party of such designation and any subsequent changes thereof;

(c) notify the other Party of any scheduled changes concerning its Designating Authority; and

(d) ensure that its Designating Authority:

   (i) has the necessary power to designate, monitor (including verification), withdraw the designation of, suspend the designation of, and lift the suspension of the designation of, the CABs that conduct conformity assessment procedures within its territory based upon the requirements set out in the other Party's mandatory requirements as specified in the relevant Sectoral Annex; and

    (ii)   consults, as necessary, with the relevant counterpart in the other Party to ensure the maintenance of confidence in conformity assessment procedures including processes. The consultations may include joint participation in audits related to conformity assessment procedures or other assessments of registered CABs, where such participation is appropriate, technically possible and within reasonable cost.

**Registration of CABs**

7.   The following procedures shall apply to the registration of a CAB:

(a)   each Party shall make a proposal that a CAB of that Party designated by its Designating Authority be registered under this Article, by presenting its proposal in writing, supported by the necessary documents, to the other Party and the TBT Joint Committee established in accordance with Article 8.7 ("TBT Joint Committee");

(b)   the other Party shall consider whether the proposed CAB complies with the stipulated and mandatory requirements specified in the relevant Sectoral Annex and communicate, to the Party making the proposal and the TBT Joint Committee in writing, the other Party's position regarding the registration of that CAB along with estimated date of registration within ninety (90) days from the date of receipt of the proposal referred to in paragraph (a). In such consideration, such other Party should assume that the proposed CAB complies with the aforementioned criteria. The TBT Joint Committee shall, within ninety (90) days from the date of receipt of the position of such other Party, decide whether to register the proposed CAB. Following the TBT Joint Committee's decision, a Party's Designating Authority shall inform the other Party about the date of registration of the proposed CAB within seven (7) days from the date of receipt of the TBT Joint Committee's decision; and

(c)   In the event that the TBT Joint Committee cannot decide to register the proposed CAB, the TBT Joint Committee may decide to conduct joint verification with or request the proposing Party to conduct a verification of the proposed CAB with the prior consent of the CAB. After the completion of such verification, the TBT Joint Committee may reconsider the proposal.

8.   The proposing Party shall provide the following information in its proposal for registration of a CAB and keep such information up-to-date:

(a)   the name and address of the CAB;

(b)   the products or processes the CAB is designated to assess;

(c)  the conformity assessment procedures the CAB is designated to conduct; and

(d)  the designation procedure and necessary information used to determine the compliance of the CAB with the stipulated requirements for designation.

9.   Each Party shall ensure that its Designating Authority withdraws the designation of its CAB registered by the Designating Authority of the other Party when its Party's Designating Authority considers that the CAB no longer complies with the stipulated and mandatory requirements of the other Party set out in the relevant Sectoral Annex. The withdrawal of the designation shall be notified in writing to the other Party and the TBT Joint Committee. Each Party shall terminate the registration of a CAB when the Designating Authority of the other Party withdraws the designation of its CAB. The date of termination of registration of the CAB shall be the date of receipt of notification for withdrawal from the other Party.

10.  Each Party shall propose the termination of the registration of its CAB when that Party considers that the CAB no longer complies with the stipulated requirements and mandatory requirements of that Party specified in the relevant Sectoral Annex. Proposal for terminating the registration of that CAB shall be made to the TBT Joint Committee and the other Party in writing. The registration of that CAB shall be terminated upon receipt by the Parties of the decision of the TBT Joint Committee.

11.  In the case of a registration of a new CAB, the other Party shall accept the results of conformity assessment procedures conducted by that CAB from the date of the registration. In the event that the registration of a CAB is terminated, the other Party shall accept the results of the conformity assessment procedures conducted by that CAB prior to the termination, without prejudice to paragraphs 18 and 19.

12.  Each Party shall notify the other Party of any scheduled changes concerning its designated CABs.

13.  The Parties shall notify the general public of the registration of CABs, on a sector-by-sector basis.

### Verification and Monitoring of Conformity Assessment Bodies

14.  Each Party shall ensure that its Designating Authority:

(a)  shall undertake through appropriate means such as audits, inspections or monitoring, that the registered CABs designated by the Party fulfill the stipulated and mandatory requirements set out in the Sectoral Annex. When applying the stipulated requirements for designation of the CABs, the Designating Authority of a Party should take into account the bodies' understanding of and experience relevant to the mandatory requirements of the other Party;

(b) shall monitor and verify that the registered CABs designated by a Party maintain the necessary technical competence to demonstrate the conformity of a product with the standards, and/or specifications to meet the mandatory requirements of the other Party. This may include participation in appropriate proficiency-testing programmes and other comparative reviews such as mutual recognition agreements between non-governmental entities, so that confidence in their technical competence to undertake the required conformity assessment is maintained; and

(c) shall exchange information concerning the procedures such as accreditation systems used to designate CABs and to ensure that the registered CABs designated by a Party are technically competent and comply with the relevant stipulated requirements.

15. When in doubt, a Party may request other designating Party in writing whether or not a registered CAB complies with the stipulated requirements for that Party's designation as set out in the mandatory requirements in the Sectoral Annex and/or request for a verification of the CAB to be conducted in accordance with that Party's mandatory requirements.

16. A Party may, with the prior consent of the other Party, participate at its own expense, in the verification process of the CAB conducted by the Designating Authority of the other Party, provided that there is prior consent of such CABs, in order to maintain a continuing understanding of that other Party's procedures for verification.

17. Each Party shall encourage its registered CABs to co-operate with the CABs of the other Party.

***Suspension and Lifting the Suspension of Designation of Conformity Assessment Bodies***

18. In case of suspension of the designation of a registered CAB, the Party, shall immediately notify the other Party and the TBT Joint Committee of the suspension. The registration of that CAB shall be suspended from the date of receipt of the decision of the TBT Joint Committee. The other Party shall accept the results of the conformity assessment procedures conducted by that CAB prior to the suspension of the designation.

19. In the case of lifting of suspension of the designation of a registered CAB, the Party shall immediately notify the other Party and the TBT Joint Committee of the lifting of suspension. The lifting of suspension of the registration of that CAB shall be effective from the date of the receipt of the decision of the TBT Joint Committee. The other Party shall accept the results of the conformity assessment procedures conducted by that CAB from the date of lifting of the suspension of the registration.

### Challenge

20. Each Party shall have the right to challenge a registered CAB's technical competence and compliance with the relevant stipulated requirements specified in the Sectoral Annex. This right shall be exercised only in exceptional circumstances and when supported by relevant expert analysis and/or evidence. A Party shall exercise this right by notifying the other Party and the TBT Joint Committee in writing.

21. Except in urgent circumstances, the Party shall, prior to a challenge exercised under paragraph 20, enter into consultations with the other Party with a view to seeking a mutually satisfactory solution. In urgent circumstances, consultations shall take place immediately after the right to challenge has been exercised. In all cases, consultations shall be conducted with a view to resolving all issues and seeking a mutually satisfactory solution within twenty (20) days or as specified in the relevant Sectoral Annex. If this is not achieved, the TBT Joint Committee shall be convened to resolve the matter.

22. Unless the TBT Joint Committee decides otherwise, the registration of the challenged CAB shall be suspended by the relevant Designating Authority for the relevant scope of designation from the date when its technical competence or compliance is challenged, until either:

    (a) the challenging Party is satisfied as to the competence and compliance of the CAB; or

    (b) the designation of that CAB has been withdrawn.

23. The Sectoral Annex may provide for additional procedures such as verification and time limits to be followed in relation to a challenge. This may involve the TBT Joint Committee being activated. Where the TBT Joint Committee decides to conduct a joint verification, it shall be conducted in a timely manner by the Parties with the participation of the Designating Authority that designated the challenged CAB and with the prior consent of the CAB. The result of such joint verification shall be discussed in the TBT Joint Committee with a view to resolving the issue within twenty (20) days or the time limit specified in the Sectoral Annex.

24. The results of conformity assessment procedures undertaken by a challenged CAB on or before the date of its suspension or withdrawal shall remain valid for acceptance for the purposes of paragraphs 4 and 5.

### ARTICLE 8.6: CONFIDENTIALITY

1. A Party shall not be required to disclose confidential proprietary information to the other Party except where such disclosure would be necessary for the other Party to demonstrate the technical competence of its designated CAB and conformity with the relevant stipulated requirements.

2. A Party shall, in accordance with its applicable laws and regulations, protect the confidentiality of any proprietary information disclosed to it in connection with conformity assessment procedures and/or designation activities.

3. Nothing in this Chapter shall be construed to require either Party to furnish or allow access to information the disclosure of which it considers would:

(a) be contrary to its essential security interests;
(b) be contrary to the public interest as determined by its domestic laws, regulations and administrative provisions;
(c) be contrary to any of its domestic laws, regulations and administrative provisions including but not limited to those protecting personal privacy or the financial affairs and accounts of individual customers of financial institutions;
(d) impede law enforcement; or
(e) prejudice legitimate commercial interests of particular public or private enterprises.

### ARTICLE 8.7: TBT JOINT COMMITTEE

1. A TBT Joint Committee shall be established on the date of entry into force of this Agreement and it shall be responsible for the effective implementation of this Chapter.

2. The TBT Joint Committee shall be led by co-chairs from both Parties. The cochairs shall be the initial contact point for the exchange of information. For this purpose, the Parties shall, through the co-chairs:

(a) broaden their exchange of information;
(b) notify any change in their mandatory requirements in accordance with their WTO obligations; and

(c) give favourable consideration to any written request for consultation. Each Party shall respond to a written request for information from the other Party in print or electronically without undue delay, and in any case within fifteen (15) days from the date of the request, at no cost or at reasonable cost.

3.　The TBT Joint Committee shall comprise representatives from both Parties.

4.　The TBT Joint Committee shall make decisions and adopt recommendations by consensus. The TBT Joint Committee shall meet, under the co-chairmanship of both Parties, when necessary to discharge its function, including upon the request of either Party.

5.　The TBT Joint Committee shall:

(a) be responsible for administering and facilitating the effective functioning of this Chapter and applicable Sectoral Annex(es), including:
  (i) facilitating the extension of this Chapter, such as the addition of new Sectoral Annexes or an increase in the scope of existing Sectoral Annexes;
  (ii) resolving any questions or disputes relating to the interpretation or application of this Chapter and applicable Sectoral Annex(es);
  (iii) deciding on the registration of a CAB, suspension of registration of a CAB, lifting of suspension of registration of a CAB, and termination of registration of a CAB with reference to Article 8.5;
  (iv) maintaining, unless the TBT Joint Committee decides otherwise, a list of registered CABs on a sector- by- sector basis;
  (v) establishing appropriate modalities of information exchange referred to in this Chapter;
  (vi) appointing experts from each Party for joint verification referred to in paragraph 16 of Article 8.5;
  (vii) discharging such other functions as provided for in this Chapter; and
  (viii) where appropriate, develop a work programme and mechanisms for co-operation in the areas of technical issues of mutual interest; and
(b) determine its own operational procedures.

6.　In case a problem is not resolved through the TBT Joint Committee, the Parties shall have final recourse to dispute settlement under Chapter 20 (Dispute Settlement).

7. The TBT Joint Committee may, where necessary, establish ad hoc groups to undertake specific tasks relating to this Chapter.

8. Any decision made by the TBT Joint Committee shall be notified promptly in writing to each Party.

9. Each Party shall, as applicable, bring into effect the relevant decisions of the TBT Joint Committee.

### ARTICLE 8.8: PRESERVATION OF REGULATORY AUTHORITY

1. Each Party retains all authority under its laws to interpret and implement its mandatory requirements.

2. This Chapter shall not:

(a) prevent a Party from adopting or maintaining, in accordance with its international rights and obligations, mandatory requirements, as appropriate to its particular national circumstances;

(b) prevent a Party from adopting mandatory requirements to determine the level of protection it considers necessary to ensure the quality of its imports, or for the protection of human, animal or plant life or health, or the environment, or for the prevention of deceptive practices or to fulfil other legitimate objectives, at the levels it considers appropriate;

(c) limit the authority of a Party to take all appropriate measures whenever it ascertains that products may not conform to its mandatory requirements. Such measures may include withdrawing the products from the market, prohibiting their placement on the market, restricting their free movement, initiating a product recall, initiating legal proceedings or otherwise preventing the recurrence of such problems including through a prohibition on imports. If a Party takes such measures, it shall notify the other Party and the TBT Joint Committee, within fifteen (15) days of taking the measures, giving its reasons;

(d) oblige a Party to accept the standards or technical regulations or mandatory requirements of the other Party;

(e) entail an obligation upon a Party to accept the results of the conformity assessment procedures and/or assessment of manufacturers or manufacturing processes of products and their mandatory requirements of any third country save where there is an expressed agreement between the Parties to do so; and

(f) be construed so as to affect the rights and obligations of either Party as a member of the WTO TBT Agreement.

## Article 8.9: Territorial Application

This Chapter shall apply to the territory of Korea and to the territory of Singapore.

## Article 8.10: Language

1.   Written communication between the Parties including between the TBT Joint Committee's co-chairs shall be in English.

2.   A Party shall make every endeavour to provide, in English and in a timely manner, information on mandatory requirements and other information or documents such as certificates, documentary evidence etc., necessary for the implementation of this Chapter and its Sectoral Annex(es).

3.   The TBT Joint Committee meetings shall be conducted in English.

4.   The decisions and records of the TBT Joint Committee shall be drawn up in English.

## Article 8.11: Sectoral Annexes

1.   The Parties shall conclude, as appropriate, Sectoral Annexes which shall provide the implementing arrangements for this Chapter.

2.   The Parties shall:

   (a)  specify and communicate to each other the applicable articles or annexes contained in the mandatory requirements set out in the Sectoral Annexes;
   (b)  exchange information concerning the implementation of the mandatory requirements specified in the Sectoral Annexes;
   (c)  notify each other of any scheduled changes in its mandatory requirements whenever they are made; and
   (d)  notify each other of any scheduled changes concerning their Designating Authorities and the registered CABs.

3.   A Sectoral Annex shall enter into force on the first day of the second month following the date on which the Parties have exchange notes confirming the completion of their respective (domestic legal) procedures for the entry into force of that Sectoral Annex.

4.   A Party may terminate a Sectoral Annex in its entirety by giving the other Party six (6) months' advance notice in writing unless otherwise stated in the relevant Sectoral Annex. However, a Party shall continue to accept the results of conformity assessment for the duration of the six-month notice period.

5.   Where urgent problems of safety, health, consumer or environment protection or national security arise or threaten to arise for a Party, that Party may suspend the operation of any Sectoral Annex, in whole or in part, immediately. In such a case, the Party shall immediately advise the other Party of the nature of the urgent problem, the products covered and the objective and rationale of the suspension.

6.   If a Party introduces new or additional conformity assessment procedures with the same product coverage to satisfy the requirements set out in the mandatory requirements specified in the Sectoral Annex, the Sectoral Annex shall be amended to set out the applicable laws, regulations and administrative provisions stipulating such new or additional conformity assessment procedures.

7.   In case of conflict between the provisions of a Sectoral Annex and this Chapter, the provisions of the Sectoral Annex shall prevail.

## CHAPTER 9
## CROSS-BORDER TRADE IN SERVICES

### ARTICLE 9.1: DEFINITIONS

For the purposes of this Chapter:

**cross-border provision of services** or **cross-border trade in services** means the provision of a service:

(a)  from the territory of a Party into the territory of the other Party;
(b)  in the territory of a Party by a person of that Party to a person of the other Party; or
(c)  by a national of a Party in the territory of the other Party;

but does not include the provision of a service in the territory of a Party by an investment as defined in Article 10.1;

**financial services** is as defined in Chapter 12 (Financial Services);

**professional services** means services, the provision of which requires specialised postsecondary education, or equivalent training or experience, and for which the right to practice is granted or restricted by a Party, but does not include services provided by trades-persons or vessel and aircraft crew members; and

**service provider of a Party** means a person of a Party that seeks to provide or provides a service[9-1].

### ARTICLE 9.2: SCOPE AND COVERAGE

1. This Chapter applies to measures adopted or maintained by a Party affecting cross-border trade in services by service providers of the other Party, including measures with respect to:

(a)  the production, distribution, marketing, sale and delivery of a service;
(b)  the purchase or use of, or payment for, a service;

---

[9-1] The Parties understand that "seeks to provide or provides a service" has the same meaning as supplies a service as used in GATS Article XXVIII(g).

(c) the access to and use of distribution and transportation systems in connection with the provision of a service;

(d) the presence in its territory of a service provider of the other Party; and

(e) the provision of a bond or other form of financial security as a condition for the provision of a service.

2. For the purposes of this Chapter, measures adopted or maintained by a Party mean measures adopted or maintained by central, or local governments and authorities or by non-governmental bodies in the exercise of any regulatory, administrative or other governmental authority delegated by central, or local governments and authorities.

3. This Chapter does not apply to:

(a) measures adopted or maintained by a Party to the extent that they are covered by Chapter 12 (Financial Services) unless specified otherwise therein;

(b) government procurement which shall be governed by Chapter 16 (Government Procurement);

(c) subsidies or grants, including government-supported loans, guarantees and insurance; or to any conditions attached to the receipt or continued receipt of such subsidies or grants, whether or not such subsidies or grants are offered exclusively to domestic services, service consumers or service suppliers;

(d) services provided in the exercise of governmental authority (such as law enforcement, correctional services, income security or insurance, social security or insurance, social welfare, public education, public training, health, and child care), provided that such services are supplied neither on a commercial basis, nor in competition with one or more service providers; and

(e) transportation and non-transportation air services, including domestic and international services, whether scheduled or non-scheduled, and related services in support of air services[9-2], other than:
(i) aircraft repair and maintenance services,
(ii) the selling and marketing of air transport services; and
(iii) computerised reservation system services.

4. Nothing in this Chapter shall be construed to impose any obligation on a Party with respect to a national of the other Party seeking access to its

---

[9-2] The Parties understand that ground handling services are part of related services in support of air services.

employment market, or employed on a permanent basis in its territory, or to confer any right on that national with respect to such access or employment.

5. Article 9.11 shall also apply to measures by a Party affecting the supply of a service in its territory by investors of the other Party or investments of investors of the other Party as defined in Article 10.1[9-3].

## ARTICLE 9.3: NATIONAL TREATMENT

1. Each Party shall accord to services and service providers of the other Party treatment no less favourable than that it accords, in like circumstances, to its own services and service providers.

2. The treatment to be accorded to a Party under paragraph 1 means, with respect to measures adopted or maintained by a local government, treatment no less favourable than the most favourable treatment accorded, in like circumstances, by that local government to service providers of the Party of which it forms a part, including itself.

## ARTICLE 9.4: LOCAL PRESENCE

Neither Party shall require a service provider of the other Party to establish or maintain a representative office or any form of enterprise, or to be resident, in its territory as a condition for the cross-border provision of a service.

## ARTICLE 9.5: MARKET ACCESS

Neither Party shall adopt or maintain, either on the basis of a regional subdivision or on the basis of its entire territory, measures that:

    (a)  limit:
        (i)   the number of service suppliers whether in the form of numerical quotas, monopolies, exclusive service suppliers or the requirement of an economic needs test;
        (ii)  the total value of service transactions or assets in the form of numerical quotas or the requirement of an economic needs test;
        (iii)  the total number of service operations or the total quantity of services output expressed in terms of designated numerical units

---

[9-3] The Parties understand that nothing in this Chapter, including this paragraph, is subject to investor-state dispute settlement pursuant to Section C of Chapter 10 (Investment).

in the form of quotas or the requirement of an economic needs test;[9-4]

(iv) the total number of natural persons that may be employed in a particular service sector or that a service supplier may employ and who are necessary for, and directly related to, the supply of a specific service in the form of numerical quotas or the requirement of an economic needs test; and

(b) restrict or require specific types of legal entity or joint venture through which a service supplier may supply a service.

## ARTICLE 9.6: NON-CONFORMING MEASURES

1. Articles 9.3, 9.4 and 9.5 do not apply to:

(a) any existing non-conforming measure that is maintained by a Party as set out in its Schedule to Annex 9A; or

(b) the continuation or prompt renewal of any non-conforming measure referred to in paragraph (a); or

(c) an amendment to any non-conforming measure referred to in paragraph (a) to the extent that the amendment does not decrease the conformity of the measure, as it existed immediately before the amendment, with Articles 9.3, 9.4 and 9.5.

2. Articles 9.3, 9.4 and 9.5 do not apply to any measure that a Party adopts or maintains with respect to sectors, subsectors or activities, as set out in its Schedule to Annex 9B.

3. Article 9.11 shall not apply to:

(a) any existing non-conforming measure that is maintained by a Party as set out in Annex 9A; or

(b) any existing or new measure that a Party adopts or maintains with respect to sectors, subsectors or activities as set out in Annex 9B.

## ARTICLE 9.7: ADDITIONAL COMMITMENTS

1. The Parties may negotiate commitments with respect to measures affecting trade in services not subject to scheduling under Article 9.6, including those

---

[9-4] This paragraph does not cover measures of a Party which limits inputs for the supply of services.

regarding qualifications, standards or licensing matters. Such commitments shall be inscribed in a Party's Schedule of specific commitments in Annex 9C.

## ARTICLE 9.8: FUTURE LIBERALISATION

1.   The Parties will, through future negotiations, to be scheduled pursuant to the Article 22.1, further deepen liberalisation with a view to reaching the reduction or elimination of the remaining restrictions scheduled in conformity with Article 9.6 and to adding additional commitments to Article 9.7, on a mutually advantageous basis and at ensuring an overall balance of rights and obligations.

2.   If a Party makes any further liberalisation of the remaining restrictions scheduled in conformity with Article 9.6 or any additional commitments scheduled in conformity with Article 9.7 by an agreement with a non-Party, it shall afford adequate opportunity to the other Party to negotiate treatment granted therein on a mutually advantageous basis and with a view to securing an overall balance of rights and obligations.

## ARTICLE 9.9: PROCEDURES

At the first or subsequent review of this Agreement pursuant to Article 22.1, the Parties shall establish procedures for:

(a)   a Party to notify and include in its relevant Schedule:
    (i)   additional commitments pursuant to Article 9.7; and
    (ii)   amendments of measures referred to in paragraph 1(c) of Article 9.6; and
(b)   consultations on non-conforming measures or additional commitments with a view to further liberalisation.

## ARTICLE 9.10: RECOGNITION

1.   For the purposes of the fulfillment of, in whole or in part, its standards or criteria for the authorisation, licensing or certification of services suppliers, and subject to the requirements in paragraph 3, a Party may recognise the education or experience obtained, requirements met, or licenses or certifications granted in the other Party. Such recognition, which may be achieved through harmonisation or otherwise, may be based upon an agreement or arrangement between the Parties, or may be accorded autonomously.

2.   A Party that is a party to an agreement or arrangement of the type referred to in paragraph 1, whether existing or future, shall afford adequate opportunity for

the other Party, if the other Party is interested, to negotiate its accession to such an agreement or arrangement or to negotiate comparable ones with it. Where a Party accords recognition autonomously, it shall afford adequate opportunity for the other Party to demonstrate that education, experience, licences, or certifications obtained or requirements met in that other Party's territory should be recognised.

3.   A Party shall not accord recognition in a manner which would constitute a means of discrimination between countries in the application of its standards or criteria for the authorisation, licensing or certification of services suppliers, or a disguised restriction on trade in services.

4.   Annex 9D applies to measures adopted or maintained by a Party relating to the licensing or certification of professional service providers.

### ARTICLE 9.11: DOMESTIC REGULATION

1.   Each Party shall ensure that all measures of general application affecting trade in services are administered in a reasonable, objective and impartial manner.

2.   Each Party shall maintain or institute as soon as practicable judicial, arbitral or administrative tribunals or procedures which provide, at the request of an affected service supplier of the other Party, for the prompt review of, and where justified, appropriate remedies for, administrative decisions affecting trade in services. Where such procedures are not independent of the agency entrusted with the administrative decision concerned, the Party shall ensure that the procedures in fact provide for an objective and impartial review.

3.   Paragraph 2 shall not be construed to require a Party to institute such tribunals or procedures where this would be inconsistent with its constitutional structure or the nature of its legal system.

4.   Where authorisation is required for the supply of a service, the competent authorities of a Party shall, within a reasonable period of time after the submission of an application considered complete under domestic laws and regulations, inform the applicant of the decision concerning the application. At the request of the applicant, the competent authorities of the Party shall provide, without undue delay, information concerning the status of the application.

5.   With the objective of ensuring that measures relating to qualification requirements and procedures, technical standards and licensing requirements do not constitute unnecessary barriers to trade in services, the Parties shall jointly review theresults of the negotiations on disciplines on these measures, pursuant to Article VI.4 of GATS, with a view to their incorporation into this Agreement.

The Parties note that such disciplines aim to ensure that such requirements are *inter alia*:

(a)  based on objective and transparent criteria, such as competence and the ability to supply the service;
(b)  not more burdensome than necessary to ensure the quality of the service;
(c)  in the case of licensing procedures, not in themselves a restriction on the supply of the service.

6.   Pending the incorporation of disciplines pursuant to pararaph 5, a Party shall not apply licensing and qualification requirements and technical standards that nullify or impair its obligations under this Chapter in a manner which:

(a)  does not comply with the criteria outlined in paragraphs 5(a), (b) or (c); and
(b)  could not reasonably have been expected of that Party at the time the obligations were undertaken.

7.   In determining whether a Party is in conformity with its obligations under paragraph 6, account shall be taken of international standards of relevant international organisations[9-5] applied by that Party.

### ARTICLE 9.12: DENIAL OF BENEFITS

Subject to prior notification and consultation in accordance with Article 19.3 and Article 20.4, a Party may deny the benefits of this Chapter to a service provider of the other Party where the Party establishes that the service is being provided by an enterprise that is owned or controlled by persons of a non-Party and that has no substantive business operations in the territory of the other Party.

### ARTICLE 9.13: MONOPOLY AND EXCLUSIVE SERVICE SUPPLIERS

1.   Each Party shall ensure that any monopoly supplier of a service in its territory does not, in the supply of the monopoly service in the relevant market, act in a manner inconsistent with the Party's obligations under Articles 9.3 and 9.5.

2.   Where a Party's monopoly supplier competes, either directly or through an affiliated company, in the supply of a service outside the scope of its monopoly rights and which is subject to that Party's obligations under Articles 9.3 and 9.5,

---

[9-5] The term "relevant international organisations" refers to international bodies whose membership is open to relevant bodies of both Parties.

the Party shall ensure that such a supplier does not abuse its monopoly position to act in its territory in a manner inconsistent with such commitments.

3. If a Party has reason to believe that a monopoly supplier of a service of the other Party is acting in a manner inconsistent with paragraph 1 or 2, it may request the other Party establishing, maintaining or authorising such supplier to provide specific information concerning the relevant operations in its territory.

4. The provisions of this Article shall also apply to cases of exclusive service suppliers, where a Party, formally or in effect, (a) authorises or establishes a small number of service suppliers and (b) substantially prevents competition among those suppliers in its territory.

### ARTICLE 9.14: MODIFICATION OR ADDITION OF RESERVATIONS

1. By giving three (3) months of written notification to the other Party, a Party may modify or add to its non-conforming measures as set out in Annex 9A and add new sectors, sub-sectors or activities to its reservations set out in Annex 9B. At the request of the other Party, it shall hold consultations with a view to reaching agreement on any necessary adjustment required to maintain the overall balance of commitments undertaken by each Party under this Agreement. If agreement is not reached between the Parties on any necessary adjustment, the matter may be referred to arbitration in accordance with Chapter 20 (Dispute Settlement).

2. Paragraph 1 shall not be construed to prejudice the right of both Parties to maintain any existing measure or adopt new measures consistent with the reservations set out in Annexes 9A and 9B.

3. Within two (2) years after the date of entry into force of this Agreement, a Party may modify or add to its reservations as set out in Annex 9A in respect of any measure inconsistent with Article 9.5 so long as such a measure has been maintained by that Party before the date of the signature of this Agreement.

### ARTICLE 9.15: PAYMENTS AND TRANSFERS

1. Subject to its reservations pursuant to Article 9.6 and except under the circumstances envisaged in Article 9.16, a Party shall not apply restrictions on international transfers and payments for current transactions.

2. Nothing in this Chapter shall affect the rights and obligations of the Parties as members of the International Monetary Fund under the Articles of Agreement of the Fund, including the use of exchange actions which are in conformity with the

Articles of Agreement, provided that a Party shall not impose restrictions on any capital transactions inconsistently with its obligations under this Chapter regarding such transactions, except under Article 9.16, or at request of the Fund.

### ARTICLE 9.16: BALANCE-OF-PAYMENTS EXCEPTION

1.    Where a Party is in serious balance of payments and external financial difficulties or threat thereof, it may, in accordance with Articles XI and XII of GATS adopt or maintain restrictions on trade in services on which it has obligations, including on payments or transfers for transactions related to such commitments. Articles XI and XII of GATS is hereby incorporated into and made part of this Agreement.

2.    The Party introducing a measure under this Article shall promptly notify the other Party.

## CHAPTER 10
## INVESTMENT

### SECTION A – DEFINITIONS

#### ARTICLE 10.1: DEFINITIONS

For the purposes of this Chapter:

**disputing investor** means an investor that makes a claim under Section C;

**disputing Party** means a Party against which a claim is made under Section C; freely usable currency means "freely usable currency" as determined by the International Monetary Fund under its Articles of Agreement and any amendments thereto;

**investment means** every kind of asset that an investor owns or controls, directly or indirectly, and that has the characteristics of an investment, such as the commitment of capital or other resources, the expectation of gains or profits or the assumption of risk[10-1]. Forms that an investment may take include, but are not limited to[10-2]:

(a) an enterprise;
(b) shares, stocks, and other forms of equity participation in an enterprise, including rights derived therefrom;
(c) bonds, debentures, loans and other debt instruments of an enterprise, including rights derived therefrom;
(d) futures, options, and other derivatives;
(e) rights under contracts, including turnkey, construction, management, production concession or revenue-sharing contracts;

---

[10-1] For clarification, investment does not mean,
(a) claims to money that arise solely from:
   (i) commercial contracts for the sale of goods or services by a national or enterprise in the territory of a Party to an enterprise in the territory of the other Party,
   (ii) the extension of credit in connection with a commercial transaction, such as trade financing, and
(b) an order entered in a judicial or administrative action and do not involve the kinds of interests set out in subparagraphs (a) to (h).

[10-2] For the purpose of this Chapter, "loans and other debt instruments" described in paragraph (c) and "claims to money and claims to any performance under contract" described in paragraph (f) of Article 10.1 refer to assets which relate to a business activity and do not refer to assets which are of a personal nature, unrelated to any business activity.

(f)   claims to money and claims to any performance under contract having an economic value;

(g)   intellectual property rights and goodwill;

(h)   rights conferred pursuant to domestic laws and regulations or contracts such as concessions, licences, authorisations and permits; and

(i)   other tangible or intangible, movable or immovable property, and related property rights, such as leases, mortgages, liens and pledges.

**investment of an investor of a Party** means an investment owned or controlled, directly or indirectly, by an investor of such a Party;

**investor of a Party** means a Party or a national or an enterprise of a Party that is seeking to make, is making, or has made, investments in the territory of the other Party;

**investor of a non-Party** means an investor other than an investor of a Party;

**transfers** means transfers and international payments;

**TRIMs Agreement** means the Agreement on Trade-Related Investment Measures, which is part of the WTO Agreement; and

**UNCITRAL Arbitration Rules** means the arbitration rules of the United Nations Commission on International Trade Law, approved by the United Nations General Assembly on December 15, 1976.

## SECTION B – INVESTMENT

### ARTICLE 10.2: SCOPE AND COVERAGE

1.   This Chapter applies to measures adopted or maintained by a Party relating to:

(a)   investors of the other Party;

(b)   investments of investors of the other Party in the territory of a Party; and

(c)   with respect to Articles 10.7[10-3] and 10.18, all the investments in the territory of the Party.

---

[10-3] This provision will be applied only when the investment of the investor of the Party suffers loss through the imposition of performance requirements to an investment of investor of a non-Party.

2.   This Chapter applies to the existing investments at the date of the entry into force of this Agreement, as well as to the investments made or acquired after this date.

3.   For the purposes of this Chapter, measures adopted or maintained by a Party mean measures adopted or maintained by central or local governments and authorities or by non-governmental bodies in the exercise of any regulatory, administrative or other governmental authority delegated by central or local governments and authorities.

4.   This Chapter does not apply to claims arising out of events which occurred, or claims which had been raised, prior to the entry into force of this Agreement.

5.   This Chapter does not apply to services supplied in the exercise of governmental authority (such as law enforcement, correctional services, income security or insurance, social security[10-4] or insurance, social welfare, public education, public training, health, and child care), provided that such services are supplied neither on a commercial basis, nor in competition with one or more service suppliers.

### ARTICLE 10.3: RELATION TO OTHER CHAPTERS

1.   In the event of any inconsistency between this Chapter and another Chapter in this Agreement, the other Chapter shall prevail to the extent of the inconsistency.

2.   The requirement by a Party that a service provider of the other Party post a bond or other form of financial security as a condition of providing a service into its territory does not of itself make this Chapter applicable to the provision of that cross-border service. This Chapter applies to that Party's treatment of the posted bond or financial security.

3.   This Chapter does not apply to measures adopted or maintained by a Party to the extent that they are covered by Chapter 12 (Financial Services) unless specified otherwise therein.

---

[10-4] For the purpose of Article 10.11, both Parties agree that social security, public retirement or compulsory savings schemes run by the government, such as the Central Provident Fund of Singapore, fall within the scope of "services supplied in the exercise of governmental authority".

### ARTICLE 10.4: NATIONAL TREATMENT

1.   Each Party shall accord to investors of the other Party treatment no less favourable than that it accords, in like circumstances, to its own investors with respect to the establishment, acquisition, expansion, management, conduct, operation, and sale or other disposition of investments in its territory.

2.   Each Party shall accord to investments of investors of the other Party treatment no less favourable than that it accords, in like circumstances, to investments in its territory of its own investors with respect to the establishment, acquisition, expansion, management, conduct, operation, and sale or other disposition of investments.

3.   The treatment to be accorded by a Party under paragraphs 1 and 2 means, with respect to a local government, treatment no less favourable than the most favourable treatment accorded, in like circumstances, by that local government to investors, and to investments of investors, of the Party of which it forms a part, including itself.

### ARTICLE 10.5: MINIMUM STANDARD OF TREATMENT

1.   Each Party shall accord to investments of investors of the other Party treatment in accordance with the customary international law minimum standard of treatment, including fair and equitable treatment and full protection and security.

2. The concepts of "fair and equitable treatment" and "full protection and security" in paragraph 1 do not require treatment in addition to or beyond that which is required by the customary international law minimum standard of treatment of aliens and do not create additional substantive rights.

  (a)  The obligation to provide "fair and equitable treatment" includes the obligation not to deny justice in criminal, civil or administrative adjudicatory proceedings.
  (b)  The obligation to provide "full protection and security" requires each Party to provide the level of police protection required under customary international law.
  (c)  The "customary international law minimum standard of treatment of aliens" refers to all customary international law principles that protect the economic rights and interests of aliens.

3.   A determination that there has been a breach of another provision of this Agreement, or of a separate international agreement, does not establish that there has been a breach of this Article.

ARTICLE **10.6:** ACCESS TO THE JUDICIAL AND ADMINISTRATIVE PROCEDURES

Each Party shall within its territory accord to investors of the other Party treatment no less favourable than the treatment which it accords in like circumstances to its own investors, with respect to access to its courts of justice and administrative tribunals and agencies in all degrees of jurisdiction both in pursuit and in defence of such investors' rights.

ARTICLE **10.7:** PERFORMANCE REQUIREMENTS

1.   Neither Party may impose or enforce any of the following requirements, or enforce any commitment or undertaking, in connection with the establishment, acquisition, expansion, management, conduct, operation, or sale or other disposition of an investment of an investor of a Party or of a non-Party in its territory:

(a)   to export a given level or percentage of goods or services;
(b)   to achieve a given level or percentage of domestic content;
(c)   to purchase, use or accord a preference to goods produced in its territory, or to purchase goods from persons in its territory;
(d)   to purchase, use or accord a preference to services provided in its territory, or to purchase services from persons in its territory;
(e)   to relate the volume or value of imports to the volume or value of exports or to the amount of foreign exchange inflows associated with such investment;
(f)   to restrict sales of goods or services in its territory that such investment produces or provides by relating such sales to the volume or value of its exports or foreign exchange earnings;
(g)   to transfer technology, a production process or other proprietary knowledge to a person in its territory, except when the requirement is imposed or the commitment or undertaking is enforced by a court, administrative tribunal or competition authority to remedy an alleged violation of competition law or to act in a manner not inconsistent with other provisions of this Agreement; or
(h)   to supply exclusively from the territory of the Party the goods that it produces or the services that it supplies to a specific regional market or to the world market.

2.   The provisions of paragraph 1 do not preclude either Party from conditioning the receipt or continued receipt of an advantage, in connection with investment and business activities in its territory of an investor of the other Party or of a non-Party, on compliance with any of the requirements set forth in paragraphs 1(d), (g) and (h).

3.   Nothing in paragraph 1 shall be construed to prevent a Party from conditioning the receipt or continued receipt of an advantage, in connection with an investment in its territory of an investor of a Party or of a non-Party, on compliance with a requirement to locate production, provide a service, train or employ workers, construct or expand particular facilities, or carry out research and development, in its territory.

4.   Provided that such measures are not applied in an arbitrary or unjustifiable manner, or do not constitute a disguised restriction on international trade or investment, nothing in paragraphs 1(b), (c) or (d) shall be construed to prevent a Party from adopting or maintaining measures, including environmental measures:

   (a) necessary to secure compliance with laws and regulations that are not inconsistent with the provisions of this Agreement;
   (b) necessary to protect human, animal or plant life or health; or
   (c) necessary for the conservation of living or non-living exhaustible natural resources.

5.   Nothing in this Article shall be construed so as to derogate from the rights and obligations of the Parties under the TRIMs Agreement.

6.   This Article does not preclude the application of any commitment, obligation or requirement between private parties, where a Party did not impose or require such commitment, undertaking or requirement.

### ARTICLE 10.8: SENIOR MANAGEMENT AND BOARDS OF DIRECTORS

1.   Neither Party may require that an enterprise of that Party that is an investment of an investor of the other Party appoint to senior management positions individuals of any particular nationality.

2.   A Party may require that a majority of the board of directors, or any committee thereof, of an enterprise of that Party that is an investment of an investor of the other Party, be of a particular nationality, or resident in the territory of the Party, provided that the requirement does not materially impair the ability of the investor to exercise control over its investment.

### ARTICLE 10.9: NON-CONFORMING MEASURES

1.   Articles 10.4, 10.7, and 10.8 shall not apply to:

   (a) any existing non-conforming measure that is maintained by a Party as set out in its Schedule to Annex 9A;

(b) the continuation or prompt renewal of any non-conforming measure referred to in paragraph (a); or

(c) an amendment to any non-conforming measure referred to in paragraph (a) to the extent that the amendment does not decrease the conformity of the measure, as it existed immediately before the amendment, with Articles 10.4, 10.7, and 10.8.

2.    Articles 10.4, 10.7 and 10.8 shall not apply to any measure that a Party adopts or maintains with respect to sectors, sub-sectors or activities, as set out in its Schedule to Annex 9B.

3.    Neither Party shall, under any measure adopted after the date of entry into force of this Agreement and covered by its Schedule to Annex 9B, require an investor of the other Party, by reason of its nationality, to sell or otherwise dispose of an investment existing at the time the measure becomes effective.

4.    Articles 10.4 and 10.8 shall not apply to:

(a) government procurement by a Party; or

(b) subsidies or grants provided by a Party, or to any conditions attached to the receipt or continued receipt of such subsidies or grants, whether or not such subsidies or grants are offered exclusively to investors of the Party or investments of investors of the Party, including government-supported loans, guarantees and insurance.

5.    Nothing in this Chapter shall be construed so as to derogate from rights and obligations under international agreements in respect of protection of intellectual property rights to which both Parties are party, including the WTO Agreement on Trade-Related Aspects of Intellectual Property Rights and other treaties concluded under the auspices of the World Intellectual Property Organization.

## ARTICLE 10.10: FUTURE LIBERALISATION

1.    If a Party makes any further liberalisation of the remaining restrictions scheduled in conformity with Article 10.9 by an agreement with a non-Party, it shall afford adequate opportunity to the other Party to negotiate treatment granted therein on a mutually advantageous basis and with a view to securing an overall balance of rights and obligations.

2.    Through the review mechanism pursuant to Article 22.1, the Parties will engage in further liberalisation with a view to reaching the reduction or elimination of the remaining restrictions scheduled in conformity with paragraphs 1 and 2 of

Article 10.9 on a mutually advantageous basis and securing an overall balance of rights and obligations.

## ARTICLE 10.11: TRANSFERS

1.  Each Party shall permit all transfers relating to an investment of an investor of the other Party to be made freely and without delay into and out of its territory. Such transfers include:

   (a) the initial capital and additional amounts to maintain or increase an investment;
   (b) profits, dividends, interest, capital gains, royalty payments, management fees, technical assistance and other fees, returns in kind and other amounts derived from the investment;
   (c) proceeds from the sale of all or any part of the investment or from the partial or complete liquidation of the investment;
   (d) payments made under a contract entered into by the investor, or its investment, including payments made pursuant to a loan agreement;
   (e) payments made pursuant to Articles 10.13 and 10.14; and
   (f) payments arising under Section C.

2.  Each Party shall permit transfers prescribed in paragraph 1 to be made in a freely usable currency at the market rate of exchange prevailing at the time of transfer.

3.  Notwithstanding paragraphs 1 and 2, a Party may prevent a transfer through the equitable, non-discriminatory and good faith application of its laws relating to:

   (a) bankruptcy, insolvency or the protection of the rights of creditors;
   (b) issuing, trading, or dealing in securities, futures, options, or derivatives;
   (c) financial reporting or record keeping of transfers when necessary to assist law enforcement or financial regulatory authorities;
   (d) criminal or penal offences; or
   (e) ensuring compliance with orders or judgments in judicial or administrative proceedings.

## ARTICLE 10.12: SAFEGUARDS

1.  A Party may, subject to paragraph 2, adopt or maintain measures inconsistent with its obligation provided for in Article 10.4 relating to cross-border capital transactions or Article 10.11:

(a) in the event of serious balance of payments or external financial difficulties or threat thereof; or

(b) where, in exceptional circumstances, payments and capital movements between the Parties cause or threaten to cause serious difficulties for the operation of monetary policy or exchange rate policy in either Party.

2. The measures referred to in paragraph 1:

(a) shall be consistent with the Articles of Agreement of the International Monetary Fund;

(b) shall not exceed those necessary to deal with the circumstances described in paragraph 1;

(c) shall be temporary and phased out progressively as the situation improves;

(d) shall promptly be notified to the other Party;

(e) shall avoid unnecessary damage to the commercial, economic and financial interests of the other Party;

(f) shall be applied on a national treatment basis; and

(g) shall ensure that the other Party is treated as favourably as any non-Party.

3. Measures adopted or maintained pursuant to paragraph 1(b) shall not exceed a period of six (6) months and may be extended through their formal reintroduction. In addition, a Party adopting such measures or any changes shall commence consultations with the other Party in order to review the restrictions adopted by it.

4. Nothing in this Chapter shall be regarded as affecting the rights enjoyed and obligations undertaken by a Party as a party to the Articles of Agreement of the International Monetary Fund.

**ARTICLE 10.13: EXPROPRIATION AND COMPENSATION**

1. Neither Party may, directly or indirectly, nationalise or expropriate an investment of an investor of the other Party in its territory, except:

(a) for a public purpose;

(b) on a non-discriminatory basis;

(c) in accordance with due process of law and Article 10.6 ; and

(d) on payment of compensation in accordance with paragraphs 2, 3 and 4.

2.   Compensation shall:

(a)  be paid without delay and be fully realisable;

(b)  be equivalent to the fair market value of the expropriated investment immediately before the expropriation took place ("date of expropriation"); and

(c)  not reflect any change in value occurring because the intended expropriation had become known earlier.

3.   If the fair market value is denominated in a freely usable currency, the compensation paid shall be no less than the fair market value on the date of expropriation, plus interest at a commercially reasonable rate for that currency, accrued from the date of expropriation until the date of payment.

4.   If the fair market value is denominated in a currency that is not freely usable, the compensation paid – converted into the currency of payment at the market rate of exchange prevailing on the date of payment – shall be no less than:

(a)  the fair market value on the date of expropriation, converted into a freely usable currency at the market rate of exchange prevailing on that date, plus

(b)  interest, at a commercially reasonable rate for that freely usable currency, accrued from the date of expropriation until the date of payment.

5.   Notwithstanding paragraphs 1, 2, 3 and 4, any measure of expropriation relating to land, which shall be as defined in the existing domestic legislation of the expropriating Party on the date of entry into force of this Agreement, shall be, for a purpose and upon payment of compensation, in accordance with the aforesaid legislation and any subsequent amendments thereto relating to the amount of compensation where such amendments follow the general trends in the market value of the land[10-5].

6.   This Article does not apply to the issuance of compulsory licences granted in relation to intellectual property rights in accordance with the TRIPS Agreement, or to the revocation, limitation, or creation of intellectual property rights, to the extent that such issuance, revocation, limitation, or creation is consistent with Chapter 17 (Intellectual Property Rights).

---

[10-5] Article 10.13 is to be interpreted in accordance with and is subjected to the letter exchange on expropriation.

**ARTICLE 10.14: LOSSES AND COMPENSATION**

1.   Investors of a Party whose investments suffer losses owing to war or other armed conflict, a state of national emergency, revolt, insurrection, riot or other similar situations, and such losses as ones resulting from requisition or destruction of property, which was not caused in combat action or was not required by the necessity of the situation, in the territory of the other Party, shall be accorded by the other Party, treatment, as regards restitution, indemnification, compensation or other forms of settlement, no less favourable than that which the other Party accords to its own investors or to investors of any non-Party, whichever is more favourable to the investors concerned.

2.   Paragraph 1 does not apply to existing measures relating to subsidies or grants, or to any conditions attached to the receipt or continued receipt of such subsidies or grants, whether or not such subsidies or grants are offered exclusively to investors of the Party or investments of investors of the Party, including government-supported loans, guarantees and insurance, that would be inconsistent with Article 10.4 but for paragraph 4(b) of Article 10.9.

**ARTICLE 10.15: SUBROGATION**

1.   Where a Party or an agency authorised by that Party has granted a contract of insurance or any form of financial guarantee against non-commercial risks with regard to an investment by one of its investors in the territory of the other Party and when payment has been made under this contract or financial guarantee by the former Party or the agency authorised by it, the latter Party shall recognise the rights of the former Party or the agency authorised by the Party by virtue of the principle of subrogation to the rights of the investor.

2.   Where a Party or the agency authorised by the Party has made a payment to its investor and has taken over rights and claims of the investor, that investor shall not, unless authorised to act on behalf of the Party or the agency authorised by the Party, making the payment, pursue those rights and claims against the other Party.

3.   Articles 10.11, 10.13 and 10.14 shall apply *mutatis mutandis* as regards payment to be made to the Party or the agency prescribed in paragraphs 1 and 2 by virtue of such recognition of rights and claims, and the transfer of such payment.

**ARTICLE 10.16: SPECIAL FORMALITIES AND INFORMATION REQUIREMENTS**

1.   Nothing in Article 10.4 shall be construed to prevent a Party from adopting or maintaining a measure that prescribes special formalities in connection with

the establishment of investments by investors of the other Party, such as the requirement that investments be legally constituted under the laws or regulations of the Party, provided that such formalities are consistent with this Chapter and do not materially impair the protections pursuant to this Chapter afforded by a Party to investors of the other Party and investments of investors of the other Party.

2.    Notwithstanding Article 10.4, a Party may require an investor of the other Party, or an investment of the investor in its territory, to provide routine information concerning that investment solely for informational or statistical purposes. The Party shall protect such business information that is confidential from any disclosure that would prejudice the competitive position of the investor or the investment. Nothing in this paragraph shall be construed to prevent a Party from otherwise obtaining or disclosing information in connection with the equitable and good faith application of its law.

### ARTICLE 10.17: DENIAL OF BENEFITS

Subject to prior notification and consultation in accordance with Articles 19.3 and 20.4, a Party may deny the benefits of this Chapter to an investor of the other Party that is an enterprise of such other Party and to investments of that investor if investors of a non-Party own or control the enterprise and the enterprise has no substantive business operations in the territory of the other Party under whose law it is constituted or organised.

### ARTICLE 10.18: ENVIRONMENTAL MEASURES

Nothing in this Chapter shall be construed to prevent a Party from adopting, maintaining or enforcing any measure otherwise consistent with this Chapter that it considers appropriate to ensure that investment activity in its territory is undertaken in a manner sensitive to environmental concerns.

### SECTION C – SETTLEMENT OF DISPUTES
### BETWEEN A PARTY AND AN INVESTOR OF THE OTHER PARTY

### ARTICLE 10. 19: SETTLEMENT OF DISPUTES BETWEEN A PARTY AND AN INVESTOR OF THE OTHER PARTY

1.    This Article shall apply to disputes between a Party and an investor of the other Party concerning an alleged breach of an obligation of the former under

this Chapter which causes loss or damage to the investor or its investment and establishes a mechanism for the settlement of investment disputes that assures both equal treatment among investors of the Parties in accordance with the principle of international reciprocity and due process before an impartial tribunal.

2.   The parties to the dispute shall initially seek to resolve the dispute by consultations and negotiations.

3.   If the dispute cannot be resolved as provided for under paragraph 2 within six (6) months from the date of a request for consultations and negotiations, and if the investor concerned has not submitted the investment dispute for resolution (a) before the courts or administrative tribunals of the disputing Party (excluding proceedings for interim measures of protection referred to in paragraph 5), or (b) in accordance with any previously agreed dispute settlement procedures, the investor concerned may submit the dispute for settlement to:

(a)   the International Centre for Settlement of Investment Disputes (ICSID), if both Parties are parties to the ICSID Convention;
(b)   arbitration under UNCITRAL Arbitration Rules; or
(c)   any other arbitral institution or in accordance with any other arbitral rules, if the parties to the dispute so agree.

4.   Each Party hereby consents to the submission of a dispute to arbitration under paragraphs 3(a) and 3(b) in accordance with the provisions of this Article, conditional upon:

(a)   the submission of the dispute to such arbitration taking place within three (3) years of the time at which the disputing investor became aware, or should reasonably have become aware, of a breach of an obligation under this Chapter and, of the loss or damage incurred by the disputing investor or its investment;
(b)   the disputing investor not being an enterprise of the disputing Party until the disputing investor refers the dispute for arbitration pursuant to paragraph 3; and
(c)   the disputing investor providing written notice, which shall be delivered at least ninety (90) days before the claim to arbitration is submitted, to the disputing Party of its intent to submit the dispute to such arbitration and which:
   (i)   nominates one (1) of the fora in paragraph 3(a), (b) or (c) as the forum for dispute settlement;
   (ii)   briefly summarises the alleged breach of the disputing Party under this Chapter (including the articles alleged to have been breached) and the loss or damage allegedly caused to the investor or its investment.

5.   Neither Party shall prevent the disputing investor from seeking interim measures of protection, not involving the payment of damages or resolution of the substance of the matter in dispute before the courts or administrative tribunals of the disputing Party, prior to the institution of proceedings before any of the dispute settlement fora referred to in paragraph 3, for the preservation of its rights and interests.

6.   Neither Party shall give diplomatic protection, or bring an international claim, in respect of a dispute which one of its investors and the other Party shall have consented to submit or have submitted to arbitration under this Article, unless such other Party has failed to abide by and comply with the award rendered in such dispute. Diplomatic protection, for the purposes of this paragraph, shall not include informal diplomatic exchanges for the sole purpose of facilitating a settlement of the dispute.

## CHAPTER 11
## TELECOMMUNICATIONS

ARTICLE 11.1: DEFINITIONS

For the purposes of this Chapter:

**cost-oriented** means based on cost, and may include a reasonable profit, and may involve different cost methodologies for different facilities or services;

**end-user means** a final consumer of or subscriber to a public telecommunications service, including a service supplier but excluding a supplier of public telecommunications transport network or services;

**essential facilities** means facilities of a public telecommunications transport network or service that:

(a)  are exclusively or predominantly provided by a single or limited number of suppliers; and
(b)  cannot feasibly be economically or technically substituted in order to provide a service;

**facilities-based suppliers** means suppliers of public telecommunications transport networks or services that are:

(a)  for Korea, telecommunications carriers provided for in Article 5 of the Telecommunications Business Act; and
(b)  for Singapore, Facilities-Based Operators;

**major supplier** means a supplier of basic telecommunications services that has the ability to materially affect the terms of participation (having regard to price and supply) in the relevant market for public telecommunications transport network or services as a result of:

(a)  control over essential facilities; or
(b)  use of its position in the market;

**network element** means a facility or equipment used in the provision of a public telecommunications service, including features, functions, and capabilities that are provided by means of such facility or equipment;

**non-discriminatory** means treatment no less favourable than that accorded to any other user of like public telecommunications transport networks or services in like circumstances;

**number portability** means the ability of end-users of public telecommunications transport network or services to retain existing telephone numbers without impairment of quality, reliability, or convenience when switching between like suppliers of public telecommunications transport network or services;

**public telecommunications transport network** means public telecommunications infrastructure that permits telecommunications between defined network termination points;

**public telecommunications transport network or services** means public telecommunications transport network and/or public telecommunications transport services;

**public telecommunications transport service** means any telecommunications transport service required by a Party, explicitly or in effect, to be offered to the public generally, including telegraph, telephone, telex and data transmission, that typically involves the real-time transmission of customer-supplied information between two or more points without any end-to-end change in the form or content of the customer's information;

service supplier means any person that supplies a service;
telecommunications means the transmission and reception of signals by any electromagnetic means; and

**user** means service consumers and service suppliers.

ARTICLE **11.2** : SCOPE AND COVERAGE[11-1]

1.   This Chapter shall apply to measures adopted or maintained by a Party that affect access to and use of, and the regulation of public telecommunications transport networks and services.

2.   This Chapter does not apply to any measure adopted or maintained by a Party relating to cable or broadcast distribution of radio or television programming.

---

[11-1] The obligations of a Party in this Chapter shall be applied in a non-discriminatory manner to suppliers of public telecommunications transport network or services of both Parties.

3.  Nothing in this Chapter shall be construed to:

    (a) require a Party to authorise a service supplier of the other Party to establish, construct, acquire, lease, operate or provide telecommunications transport networks or services; or
    (b) require a Party (or require a Party to compel any service supplier) to establish, construct, acquire, lease, operate or provide telecommunications transport networks or services not offered to the public generally.

ARTICLE 11.3: ACCESS TO AND USE OF PUBLIC TELECOMMUNICATIONS TRANSPORT NETWORKS AND SERVICES

1.  Each Party shall ensure that service suppliers of the other Party have access to and use of any public telecommunications transport network and service, including private leased circuits, offered in its territory or across its borders on reasonable, nondiscriminatory, timely and transparent terms and conditions, including as those set out in paragraphs 2, 3, 4, 5 and 6.

2.  Each Party shall ensure that service suppliers of the other Party are permitted to:

    (a) purchase or lease, and attach terminal or other equipment that interfaces with the public telecommunications transport network;
    (b) interconnect leased or owned circuits with public telecommunications transport networks and services in the territory, of that Party, or with circuits leased or owned by another service supplier;
    (c) perform switching, signaling and processing functions;
    (d) use operating protocols of their choice, other than as necessary to ensure the availability of telecommunications transport networks and services to the public generally; and
    (e) provide services to individual or multiple end-users over any leased or owned circuit(s) to the extent that the scope and type of such services are not inconsistent with each Party's domestic laws and regulations.

3.  Each Party shall ensure that service suppliers of the other Party may use public telecommunications transport networks and services for the movement of information in its territory or across its borders, including for intra-corporate communications, and for access to information contained in data-bases or otherwise stored in machine-readable form in the territory of the other Party.

4.   Notwithstanding the preceding paragraph, a Party may take such measures as are necessary to ensure the security and confidentiality of messages, or to protect the privacy of personal data of end-users, subject to the requirement that such measures are not applied in a manner which would constitute a means of arbitrary or unjustifiable discrimination or a disguised restriction on trade in services.

5.   Each Party shall ensure that no condition is imposed on access to and use of public telecommunications transport networks and services, other than that necessary to:

(a)   safeguard the public service responsibilities of suppliers of public tele-communications transport networks and services, in particular their ability to make their networks or services available to the public generally; or

(b)   protect the technical integrity of public telecommunications transport networks and services.

6.   Provided that they satisfy the criteria set out in paragraph 5, conditions for access to and use of public telecommunications transport networks and services may include:

(a)   a requirement to use specified technical interfaces, including interface protocols, for interconnection with such networks or services;

(b)   requirements, where necessary, for the inter-operability of such services;

(c)   type approval of terminal or other equipment which interfaces with the network and technical requirements relating to the attachment of such equipment to such networks; or

(d)   notification, registration and licensing.

### ARTICLE 11.4: CONDUCT OF MAJOR SUPPLIERS

#### Treatment by Major Suppliers

1.   Each Party shall ensure that any major supplier in its territory accords facilities-based suppliers, licensed in its territory, of the other Party treatment no less favourable than such major supplier accords to itself, its subsidiaries, its affiliates, or any nonaffiliated service supplier, provided they are facilities-based suppliers, regarding:

(a)   the availability, provisioning, rates, or quality of like public telecommunications transport network or services; and

(b) the availability of technical interfaces necessary for interconnection.

When necessary, a Party shall assess such treatment on the basis of whether such suppliers of public telecommunications transport network or services, subsidiaries, affiliates, and non-affiliated service suppliers are in like circumstances.

## *Competitive Safeguards*

2.  (a) Each Party shall maintain appropriate measures for the purpose of preventing suppliers of public telecommunications transport network or services who, alone or together, are a major supplier in its territory from engaging in or continuing anti-competitive practices.

    (b) For the purposes of paragraph (a), anti-competitive practices include:
        (i) engaging in anti-competitive cross-subsidisation;
        (ii) using information obtained from competitors with anti-competitive results;
        (iii) not making available, on a timely basis, to suppliers of public telecommunications transport network or services, technical information about essential facilities and commercially relevant information that is necessary for them to provide public telecommunications transport network or services; and
        (iv) pricing services in a manner that gives rise to unfair competition.

## *Unbundling of Network Elements*

3.  (a) Each Party shall ensure that major suppliers in its territory provide to facilities-based suppliers, licensed in its territory, of the other Party access to network elements for the provision of public telecommunications transport network or services at any technically feasible point, on an unbundled basis, in a timely fashion; and on terms, conditions, and cost-oriented rates that are reasonable, transparent, and non-discriminatory.

    (b) Each Party may determine, in accordance with its domestic laws and regulations, which network elements it requires major suppliers in its territory to provide access to in accordance with paragraph (a) on the basis of the technical feasibility of unbundling and the state of competition in the relevant market.

## *Co-Location*

4.  (a) Each Party shall ensure that major suppliers in its territory provide to facilities-based suppliers, licensed in its territory, of the other Party

physical co-location of equipment necessary for interconnection or access to unbundled network elements in a timely fashion and on terms, conditions, and cost-oriented rates that are reasonable, transparent, and nondiscriminatory.

(b) Where physical co-location under paragraph (a) is not practical for technical reasons or because of space limitations, each Party shall ensure that major suppliers co-operate with facilities-based suppliers to find alternatives, which could include site inspections of co-location premises, in accordance with each Party's domestic laws and regulations.

(c) Each Party may determine, in accordance with its domestic laws and regulations, which premises in its territory shall be subject to paragraphs (a) and (b).

### Resale

5. (a) Each Party shall ensure that major suppliers in its territory do not impose unreasonable or discriminatory conditions, limitations or rates on the resale of public telecommunications transport network or services that the major supplier provides at retail to end-users.

(b) Each Party may determine, in accordance with its domestic laws and regulations, the type and scope of resale in its territory.

### Poles, Ducts, and Conduits

6. (a) Each Party shall ensure that major suppliers in its territory provide access to poles, ducts, conduits, or any other structures deemed necessary by the Party, which are owned or controlled by such major suppliers to facilities-based suppliers, licensed in its territory, of the other Party:
   (i)  in a timely fashion; and
   (ii) on terms, conditions, and cost-oriented rates that are reasonable, transparent, and non-discriminatory.

(b) Each Party may determine, in accordance with its domestic laws and regulations, the poles, ducts, conduits or other structures to which it requires major suppliers in its territory to provide access under paragraph (a) on the basis of the state of competition in the relevant market.

*Number Portability*

7.   Each Party shall ensure that major suppliers in its territory provide number portability, for those services designated by that Party, to the extent technically feasible, on a timely basis and on reasonable terms and conditions.

*Interconnection*

8.   (a)   *General Terms and Conditions*

*Interconnection to be Ensured*

Each Party shall ensure interconnection between a facilities-based supplier and any other facilities-based supplier or a services-based supplier to the extent provided for in its laws and regulations.

*Interconnection with Major Suppliers*

Each Party shall ensure that a major supplier is required to provide interconnection at any technically feasible point in the network. Such interconnection is provided:

(i)   under non-discriminatory terms, conditions (including technical standards and specifications) and rates and of a quality no less favourable than that provided for its own like services, or for like services of non-affiliated service suppliers or for like services of its subsidiaries or other affiliates;

(ii)   in a timely fashion, on terms, conditions (including technical standards and specifications) and cost-oriented rates that are transparent, reasonable, having regard to economic feasibility, and sufficiently unbundled so that the supplier need not pay for network components or facilities that it does not require for the services to be provided; and

(iii)   upon request, at points in addition to the network termination points offered to the majority of users, subject to charges that reflect the cost of construction of necessary additional facilities.

(b)   *Transparency of interconnection arrangements*

Each Party shall ensure that a major supplier will make publicly available either its interconnection agreements or a reference interconnection offer.

(c)  *Public Availability of the Procedures for Interconnection Negotiations*

Each Party shall make publicly available the applicable procedures for inter-connection negotiations with major suppliers in its territory.

(d)  *Public Availability of Interconnection Agreements Concluded with Major Suppliers*

    (i)   Each Party shall require major suppliers in its territory to file all their inter-connection agreements with its telecommunications regulatory body.

    (ii)  Each Party shall make available to suppliers of public telecom-munications transport network or services which are seeking inter-connection, interconnection agreements between a major supplier in its territory and any other supplier of public telecommunications transport network or services in such territory.

(e)  *Resolution of Interconnection Disputes*

Each Party shall ensure that suppliers of public telecommunications transport network or services of the other Party, that have requested interconnection with a major supplier in the Party's territory have recourse to a telecommunications regulatory body to resolve disputes regarding the terms, conditions, and rates for interconnection within a reasonable and publicly available period of time.

## Provisioning and Pricing of Leased Circuits Services[11-2]

9.   Each Party shall ensure that major suppliers of leased circuits services in its territory provide service suppliers of the other Party leased circuits services that are public telecommunications transport network or services, on terms and conditions, and at rates that are reasonable, non-discriminatory, timely, and transparent.

## ARTICLE 11.5: INDEPENDENT REGULATORS

1.   Each Party shall ensure that its telecommunications regulatory body is separate from, and, not accountable to, any supplier of public telecommunications transport network or services.

2.   Each Party shall ensure that the decisions of, and procedures used by its telecom-munications regulatory body are impartial with respect to all market participants.

---

[11-2] The obligation under this article is not an obligation to provide leased circuits as an unbundled network element.

## ARTICLE 11.6: UNIVERSAL SERVICE

Each Party shall administer any universal service obligation that it maintains in a transparent, nondiscriminatory, and competitively neutral manner and shall ensure that its universal service obligation is not more burdensome than necessary for the kind of universal service that it has defined.

## ARTICLE 11.7: LICENSING PROCESS

1.   When a Party requires a supplier of public telecommunications transport network or services to have a licence, the Party shall make publicly available:

(a)   all the licensing criteria and procedures it applies;
(b)   the period of time normally required to reach a decision concerning an application for a licence; and
(c)   the terms and conditions of all licences.

2.   Each Party shall ensure that an applicant receives, upon request, the reasons for the denial of a licence.

## ARTICLE 11.8: ALLOCATION AND USE OF SCARCE RESOURCES[11-3]

1.   Each Party shall administer its procedures for the allocation and use of scarce resources, including frequencies, numbers, and rights of way, in an objective, timely, transparent, and non-discriminatory fashion.

2.   Each Party shall make publicly available the current state of allocated frequency bands but shall not be required to provide detailed identification of frequencies assigned or allocated by each government for specific government uses.

## ARTICLE 11.9: ENFORCEMENT

Each Party shall ensure that its telecommunications regulatory body maintains appropriate procedures and authority to enforce domestic measures relating

---

[11-3] The Parties understand that decisions on allocating and assigning spectrum, and frequency management are not measures that are *per se* inconsistent with Article 9.5 and Article 10.7. Accordingly, each Party retains the right to exercise its spectrum and frequency management policies, which may affect the number of suppliers of public telecommunications services, provided that this is done in a manner that is consistent with the provisions of this Agreement. The Parties also retain the right to allocate frequency bands taking into account existing and future needs.

to the obligations under this Chapter. Such procedures and authority shall include the ability to impose effective sanctions, which may include financial penalties, corrective orders, or modification, suspension, and revocation of licences.

## ARTICLE 11.10: RESOLUTION OF DOMESTIC TELECOMMUNICATIONS DISPUTES

### *Recourse*

1.   Each Party shall ensure that suppliers of public telecommunications transport networks or services of the other Party have timely recourse to a telecommunications regulatory body or other relevant body to resolve disputes arising under domestic measures addressing a matter set out in this Chapter.

### *Reconsideration*

2.   Each Party shall ensure that any supplier of public telecommunications transport networks or services aggrieved by the determination or decision of the telecommunications regulatory body may petition that body for reconsideration of that determination or decision. Neither Party may permit such a petition to constitute grounds for non-compliance with such determination or decision of the telecommunications regulatory body unless an appropriate authority stays such determination or decision.

### *Appeal*

3.   Each Party shall ensure that any supplier of public telecommunications transport networks or services aggrieved by a determination or decision of the telecommunications regulatory body has the opportunity to appeal such determination or decision to an independent judicial or administrative authority.

## ARTICLE 11.11: TRANSPARENCY

Each Party shall ensure that:

   (a)  rulemakings, including the basis for such rulemakings, of its telecommunications regulatory body are published or otherwise made available to interested persons in a reasonable period of time;
   (b)  interested persons are provided with adequate advance public notice of and the opportunity to comment on any rulemaking proposed by the telecommunications regulatory body[11-4]; and

(c) its measures relating to public telecommunications transport network or services are made publicly available, including:
   (i) tariffs and other terms and conditions of service;
   (ii) specifications of technical interfaces;
   (iii) conditions applying to attachment of terminal or other equipment to the public telecommunications transport network;
   (iv) notification, permit, registration, or licensing requirements, if any; and
   (v) information on bodies responsible for preparing, amending, and adopting standards- related measures is made publicly available.

ARTICLE 11.12: RELATION TO OTHER CHAPTERS

In the event of any inconsistency between this Chapter and another Chapter in this Agreement, this Chapter shall prevail to the extent of the inconsistency.

ARTICLE 11.13: RELATION TO INTERNATIONAL ORGANISATIONS AND AGREEMENTS

The Parties recognise the importance of international standards for global compatibility and inter-operability of telecommunication networks or services and undertake to promote those standards through the work of relevant international bodies, including the International Telecommunication Union and the International Organization for Standardization.

---

[11-4] The obligations under paragraph (b) will be applied in accordance with each Party's domestic laws and regulations.

## CHAPTER 12
## FINANCIAL SERVICES

### ARTICLE 12.1: SCOPE AND COVERAGE

1.   This Chapter applies to measures adopted or maintained by a Party relating to:

  (a)  financial institutions of the other Party;
  (b)  investors of the other Party, and investments of such investors, in financial institutions in the Party's territory; and
  (c)  trade in financial services.

2.   Chapters 9 (Cross-Border Trade in Services) and 10 (Investment) apply to measures described in paragraph 1 only to the extent that such Chapters or Articles of such Chapters are incorporated into this Chapter. For this purpose:

  (a)  Articles 9.12, 9.15, 10.11, 10.12, 10.13, 10.16, 10.17 and 10.18 are hereby incorporated into and made a part of this Chapter;
  (b)  As for Articles 9.16 and 10.12, in the event of any inconsistency between Chapter 9 (Cross-Border Trade in Services) and Chapter 10 (Investment) in this Agreement, Chapter 10 shall prevail to the extent of the inconsistency; and
  (c)  Section C of Chapter 10 (Investment) is hereby incorporated into and made a part of this Chapter solely for claims that a Party has breached Articles 10.11, 10.13, 10.16 and 10.17, as incorporated into this Chapter.

3.   This Chapter does not apply to measures adopted or maintained by a Party relating to:

  (a)  activities conducted by a central bank or monetary authority or by any other public entity in pursuit of monetary or exchange rate policies;
  (b)  activities or services forming part of a public retirement plan or statutory system of social security; or
  (c)  activities or services conducted for the account or with the guarantee or using the financial resources of the Party, including its public entities,

except that this Chapter shall apply if a Party allows any of the activities or services referred to in subparagraphs (a), (b) or (c) to be conducted by its financial institutions in competition with a public entity or a financial institution.

4.   This Chapter does not apply to laws, regulations or requirements governing the procurement by government agencies of financial services purchased for

governmental purposes and not with a view to commercial resale or use in the supply of services for commercial sale.

### Article 12.2: National Treatment

1.   In the sectors inscribed in its Schedule in Annex 12A, and subject to any conditions and qualifications set out therein, each Party shall accord to financial services and financial service suppliers of the other Party, in like circumstance, in respect of all measures affecting the supply of financial services, treatment no less favourable than that it accords to its own like financial services and financial service suppliers.

2.   In the sectors inscribed in its Schedule in Annex 12A, and subject to any conditions and qualifications set out therein, each Party shall accord to the investors of the other Party, in like circumstances, in respect of the establishment, acquisition, expansion, management, conduct, operation and sale or other disposition of financial institutions and investments in financial institutions in its territory, treatment no less favourable than that it accords to its own like investors.

3.   In the sectors inscribed in its Schedule in Annex 12A, and subject to any conditions and qualifications set out therein, each Party shall accord to the financial institutions of the other Party and to investments of investors of the other Party in financial institutions, in like circumstances, in respect of establishment, acquisition, expansion, management, conduct, operation and sale or other disposition of financial institutions and investments, treatment no less favourable than that it accords to its own like financial institutions, and to investments of its own like investors in financial institutions.

4.   A Party may meet the requirement of paragraphs 1, 2 and 3 by according to financial services and financial service suppliers of the other Party, investors of the other Party, financial institutions of the other Party and to investments of investors of the other Party in financial institutions, as the case may be, in like circumstance, either formally identical treatment or formally different treatment to that it accords to its own like financial services and financial service suppliers, its own like investors, its own like financial institutions and investments of its own like investors in financial institutions, respectively.

5.   Formally identical or formally different treatment shall be considered to be less favourable if it modifies the conditions of competition in favour of financial services and financial service suppliers of a Party, investors of a Party, financial institutions of a Party and to investments of investors of a Party in financial institutions compared to like financial services or financial service suppliers of the other Party, like investors of the other Party, like financial institutions of the other

Party and investments of like investors of the other Party in financial institutions in like circumstance.

## ARTICLE 12.3: MARKET ACCESS

1.   With respect to market access through the modes of supply identified in the definition of trade in financial services in Article 12.15, each Party shall accord financial services and financial service suppliers of the other Party treatment no less favourable than that provided for under the terms, limitations and conditions agreed and specified in its schedule in Annex 12A.

2.   In sectors where market-access commitments are undertaken, the measures which a Party shall not maintain or adopt either on the basis of regional subdivision or on the basis of its entire territory, unless otherwise specified in its Schedule in Annex 12A, are defined as:

(a)  limitations on the number of financial institutions whether in the form of numerical quotas, monopolies, exclusive service providers or the requirements of an economic needs test;

(b)  limitations on the total value of financial service transactions or assets in the form of numerical quotas or the requirement of an economic needs test;

(c)  limitations on the total number of financial service operations or the total quantity of financial services output expressed in terms of designated numerical units in the form of quotas or the requirement of an economic needs test;

(d)  limitations on the total number of natural persons that may be employed in a particular financial service sector or that a financial institution may employ and who are necessary for, and directly related to, the supply of a specific financial service in the form of a numerical quota or the requirement of an economic needs test;

(e)  measures which restrict or require specific types of legal entity or joint venture through which a financial institution may supply a service; and

(f)  limitations on the participation of foreign capital in terms of maximum percentage limit on foreign shareholding or the total value of individual or aggregate foreign investment.

## ARTICLE 12.4: SCHEDULE OF SPECIFIC COMMITMENTS

1.   Each Party shall set out in a schedule the specific commitments it undertakes under Articles 12.2 and 12.3. With respect to sectors where such commitments are undertaken, each Schedule shall specify:

(a)  terms, limitations and conditions on market access;

(b)  conditions and qualifications on national treatment;

(c) undertakings relating to additional commitments;

(d) where appropriate, the time-frame for implementation of such commitments.

2. Measures inconsistent with both Articles 12.2 and 12.3 shall be inscribed in the column relating to Article 12.3. In this case the inscription will be considered to provide a condition or qualification to Article 12.2 as well.

3. Schedules of specific commitments shall be annexed to this Agreement as Annex12A and shall form an integral part thereof.

## ARTICLE 12.5: TRANSPARENCY

1. Each Party commits to promote regulatory transparency in financial services. Accordingly, the Parties shall consult with the goal of promoting objective and transparent regulatory processes in each Party, taking into account

(a) the work undertaken by the Parties in GATS and the Parties' work in other fora relating to trade in financial services; and

(b) the importance of regulatory transparency of identifiable policy objectives and clear and consistently applied regulatory processes that are communicated or otherwise made available to the public.

2. Each Party shall publish promptly and, except in emergency situations, at latest by the time of their entry into force, all relevant regulatory measures of general application which pertain to or affect the operation of this Agreement. International agreements pertaining to or affecting trade in financial services to which a Party is a signatory shall also be published.

3. Where publication as referred to paragraph 2 is not practicable, such information shall be made otherwise publicly available.

4. Each Party shall respond promptly to all requests by the other Party for specific information of its regulatory measures of general application or international agreements within the meaning of paragraph 2. Each Party shall also establish one or more enquiry points to provide specific information to the other Party, upon request, on all such matters.

## ARTICLE 12.6: EXCEPTIONS

1. Nothing in this Agreement shall be construed to prevent a Party from adopting or maintaining measures for prudential reasons, including for the protection of

investors, depositors, policy holders or persons to whom a fiduciary duty is owed by a financial service supplier, or to ensure the integrity and stability of a Party's financial system. Where such measures do not conform with the provisions of this Agreement, they shall not be used as a means of avoiding the Party's commitments or obligations under such provisions.

2.   Nothing in this Chapter or Chapters 10 (Investment), 11 (Telecommunications), or 14 (Electronic Commerce) applies to non-discriminatory measures of general application taken by any public entity in pursuit of monetary and related credit policies or exchange rate policies. This paragraph shall not affect a Party's obligations under Articles 9.15, 10.7 or 10.11.

3.   Notwithstanding Articles 9.15 and 10.11, as incorporated into this Chapter, a Party may prevent or limit transfers by a financial institution or financial service supplier to, or for the benefit of, an affiliate of or a person related to such institution or supplier, through the equitable, non-discriminatory and good faith application of measures relating to maintenance of the safety, soundness, integrity or financial responsibility of financial institutions or financial service suppliers. This paragraph does not prejudice any other provision of this Agreement that permits a Party to restrict transfers.

4.   For greater certainty, nothing in this Chapter shall be construed to prevent the adoption or enforcement by a Party of measures necessary to secure compliance with laws or regulations that are not inconsistent with this Chapter including those relating to the prevention of deceptive and fraudulent practices or to deal with the effects of a default on financial services contracts, subject to the requirement that such measures are not applied in a manner which would constitute a means of arbitrary or unjustifiable discrimination between countries where like conditions prevail, or a disguised restriction on investment in financial institutions or cross-border trade in financial services.

### ARTICLE 12.7: DOMESTIC REGULATION

In sectors where specific commitments are undertaken in its schedule to Annex 12A each Party shall ensure that all measures of general application to which this Chapter applies are administered in a reasonable, objective and impartial manner.

### ARTICLE 12.8: TREATMENT OF CERTAIN INFORMATION

Nothing in this Chapter shall require a Party to furnish confidential information, the disclosure of which would impede law enforcement or otherwise be contrary to the public interest, or which would prejudice legitimate commercial interests of particular enterprises, public or private.

ARTICLE **12.9:** RECOGNITION

1.   A Party may recognise the prudential measures of any international regulatory body or non-Party in determining how the Party's measures relating to financial servces shall be applied. Such recognition, which may be achieved through harmonisation or otherwise, may be based upon an agreement or arrangement with the international regulatory body or non-Party concerned or may be accorded autonomously.

2.   A Party that is a party to such an agreement or arrangement referred to in paragraph 1, whether future or existing, shall afford adequate opportunity for the other Party to negotiate its accession to such agreements or arrangements, or to negotiate comparable ones with it, under circumstances in which there would be equivalent regulation, oversight, implementation of such regulation, and if appropriate, procedures concerning the sharing of information between the parties to the agreement or arrangement. Where a Party accords recognition autonomously, it shall afford adequate opportunity for the other Party to demonstrate that such circumstances exist.

ARTICLE **12.10:** FINANCIAL SERVICES COMMITTEE

1.   The Parties hereby establish a Financial Services Committee. The principal representative of each Party shall be an official of the Party's authority responsible for financial services.

2.   The Financial Services Committee shall:

   (a)   supervise the implementation of this Chapter and its further elaboration;
   (b)   consider issues regarding financial services that are referred to it by a Party; and
   (c)   participate in the dispute settlement procedures in accordance with Article 12.12.

3.   The Financial Services Committee shall meet one year after this Agreement has entered into force and thereafter as otherwise agreed by both Parties, to assess the functioning of this Agreement as it applies to financial services.

ARTICLE **12.11:** CONSULTATIONS

1.   A Party may request consultations with the other Party regarding any matter arising under this Agreement that affects financial services. The other Party shall

give sympathetic consideration to the request. The Parties shall report the results of their consultations to the Financial Services Committee.

2.    Consultation under this Article shall include officials of the authority responsible for financial services.

### Article 12.12: Dispute Settlement

1.    Relevant Articles in Chapter 20 (Dispute Settlement) applies as modified by this Article to the settlement of disputes arising under this Chapter.

2.    For the purposes of this Article, consultations held pursuant to Article 12.11 shall be deemed to be consultations within the meaning of Article 20.4.

3.    When a Party claims that a dispute arises under this Chapter, Article 20.7 shall apply, except that:

   (a)   where the Parties so agree, the panel shall be composed entirely of panelists meeting the qualifications in paragraph 4;
   (b)   in any other case,
      (i)    each Party may select panelists meeting the qualifications set out in paragraph 4 or paragraph 4 of Article 20.7; and
      (ii)   if the Party complained against invokes Article 12.6, the chair of panel shall meet the qualifications set out in paragraph 4, unless the parties agree otherwise.

4.    Financial services panelists shall:

   (a)   have expertise or experience in financial services law or practice, which may include the regulation of financial institutions;
   (b)   be chosen strictly on the basis of objectivity, reliability and sound judgment; and
   (c)   meet the qualifications set out in paragraph 4 and paragraph 4 of Article 20.7.

5.    Notwithstanding Article 20.14, where a panel finds a measure to be inconsistent with this Agreement and the measure under dispute affects:

   (a)   only the financial services sector, the complaining Party may suspend benefits only in the financial services sector;
   (b)   the financial services sector and any other sector, the complaining Party may suspend benefits in the financial services sector that have an effect

equivalent to the effect of the measure in the Party's financial services sector; or

(c) only a sector other than the financial services sector, the complaining Party may not suspend benefits in the financial services sector.

### ARTICLE 12.13: INVESTMENT DISPUTES IN FINANCIAL SERVICES

1. Where an investor of a Party submits a claim under Section C in Chapter 10 (Investment) against the other Party and the respondent invokes Article 10.12 or 12.6, on request of the respondent, the tribunal shall refer the matter in writing to the Financial Services Committee for a decision. The tribunal may not proceed pending receipt of a decision or report under this Article.

2. In a referral pursuant to paragraph 1, the Financial Services Committee shall decide the issue of whether and to what extent Article 10.12 or 12.6 is a valid defence to the claim of the investor. The Financial Services Committee shall transmit a copy of its decision to the tribunal. The decision shall be binding on the tribunal.

3. Where the Financial Services Committee has not decided the issue within sixty (60) days of the receipt of the referral under paragraph 1, the respondent or the Party of the claimant may request the establishment of a panel under relevant Articles in Chapter 20 (Dispute Settlement). The panel shall be constituted in accordance with Article 12.12. The panel shall transmit its final report to the Financial Services Committee and to the tribunal. The report shall be binding on the tribunal.

4. Where no request for the establishment of a panel pursuant to paragraph 3 has been made within ten (10) days of the expiration of the 60-day period referred to in paragraph 3, a tribunal may proceed to decide the matter.

5. For the purposes of this Article, tribunal means a tribunal established pursuant to Article 10.19.

### ARTICLE 12.14: MODIFICATION OF SCHEDULES

The Parties shall, on the request in writing by either Party, hold consultations to consider any modification or withdrawal of a commitment in the Schedule of specific commitments on trade in financial services. Such consultations shall be held within three months after the requesting Party makes such a request. In such consultations, the Parties shall aim to ensure that a general level of mutually advantageous commitments not less favourable to trade than that provided for in the Schedule of specific commitments in Annex 12A prior to such consultations is maintained.

## ARTICLE 12.15: DEFINITIONS

For the purposes of this Chapter:

**trade in financial services** means the supply of a financial service:

(a) from the territory of a Party into the territory of the other Party;
(b) in the territory of a Party by a person of that Party to the financial service consumer of the other Party;
(c) by a financial service supplier of a Party, through commercial presence in the territory of the other Party;
(d) by a financial service supplier of a Party, through presence of natural persons of that Party in the territory of the other Party;

**commercial presence** means any type of business or professional establishment, including through:

(a) the constitution, acquisition or maintenance of a juridical person; or
(b) the creation or maintenance of a branch or a representative office, within the territory of a Party for the purpose of supplying a service;

**financial institution** means any financial intermediary or other institution, that is authorised to do business and regulated or supervised as a financial institution under the law of the Party in whose territory it is located;

**financial institution** of the other Party means a financial institution, including a branch, located in the territory of a Party that is controlled by persons of the other Party;

**financial service** means a service of a financial nature, including insurance, and a service incidental or auxiliary to a service of a financial nature. Financial services shall include the activities as stated in Annex 12B;

**financial service consumer** means any person that receives or uses a financial service;

**financial service supplier of a Party** means any natural or juridical person authorised by the law of a Party that is engaged in the business of supplying financial services through the trade in financial services.

**investment** means "investment" as defined in Chapter 10 (Investment), except that, with respect to "loans" and "debt instruments" referred to in that Chapter:

(a) a loan to or debt instrument issued by a financial institution is an investment only where it is treated as regulatory capital by the Party in whose territory the institution is located; and

(b) a loan granted by or debt instrument owned by a financial institution, other than a loan to or debt instrument of a financial institution referred to in subparagraph (a), is not an investment;

**investor of a Party** means a Party or state enterprise thereof, or a person of that Party, that attempts to make, is making, or has made an investment in the territory of the other Party; provided, however, that a natural person who is a dual national shall be deemed to be exclusively a national of the State of his/her dominant and effective nationality;

**juridical person** means any legal entity duly constituted or otherwise organised under applicable law, whether for profit or otherwise, and whether privately-owned or governmentally-owned, including any corporation, trust, partnership, joint venture, sole proprietorship or association, or a branch of a financial institution constituted or otherwise organised under the law of a non-Party that is registered or set up in the territory of a Party and carrying out business activities there;

**juridical person of the other Party** means a juridical person which is either:

(a) constituted or otherwise organised under the law of the other Party and, for greater certainty, includes a branch of a financial institution of a non-Party; and is engaged in substantive business operations in the territory of the other Party; or

(b) in the case of the supply of a service through commercial presence, owned or controlled by:

(i) natural persons of the other Party; or

(ii) juridical persons of the other Party identified under subparagraph (a);

**natural person of a Party** means a natural person who resides in the territory of the Party or elsewhere and who under the law of that Party:

(a) is a national of that Party; or

(b) has the right of permanent residence in that Party;

**person of a Party** means either a natural person or a juridical person;

**public entity** means:

(a)   a government, a central bank or a monetary authority of a Party, or an entity owned or controlled by a Party, that is principally engaged in carrying out governmental functions or activities for governmental purposes, not including an entity principally engaged in supplying financial services on commercial terms; for greater certainty, a public entity shall not be considered a designated monopoly or a public enterprise for purposes of Chapter 15 (Competition); or

(b)   a private entity, performing functions normally performed by a central bank or monetary authority, when exercising those functions;

**authority responsible for financial services** means:

(a)   for Korea, the Ministry of Finance and Economy; and

(b)   for Singapore, the Monetary Authority of Singapore.

## CHAPTER 13
## TEMPORARY ENTRY OF BUSINESS PERSONS


ARTICLE **13.1:** DEFINITIONS

For the purposes of this Chapter:

**business person** means a national of a Party who is engaged in trade in goods, the provision of services or the conduct of investment activities;

**business visitors** means nationals of either Party who are:

(a) service sellers;
(b) short-term service suppliers;
(c) investors of a Party or employees of an investor who are managers, executives or specialists as defined in relation to intra-corporate transferees in a Party's Schedule of Specific Commitments to GATS seeking temporary entry to establish an investment; or
(d) seeking temporary entry for the purposes of negotiating the sale of goods where such negotiations do not involve direct sales to the general public;

**service seller** means a national of a Party who is a sales representative of a service supplier of that Party and is seeking temporary entry to the other Party for the purpose of negotiating the sale of services for that service supplier, where such a representative will not be engaged in making direct sales to the general public or in supplying services directly;

**short-term service suppliers** means persons who:

(a) are employees of a service supplier or an enterprise of a Party not having a commercial presence or investment in the other Party, which has concluded a service contract with a service supplier or an enterprise engaged in substantive business operations in the other Party;
(b) have been employees of the service supplier or enterprise for a time period of not less than one year immediately preceding an application for admission for temporary entry;
(c) are managers, executives or specialists as defined in relation to intra-corporate transferees in a Party's Schedule of Specific Commitments to GATS;
(d) are seeking temporary entry to the other Party for the purpose of providing a service as a professional in the following service sectors on behalf of the service supplier or enterprise which employs them:

    (i)   professional services;
    (ii)  computer and related services;
    (iii) telecommunication services;
    (iv) financial services; or
    (v)  tour guides and translators; and

  (e)  satisfy any other requirements under the domestic laws and regulations of the other Party to provide such services in the territory of that Party; and

**temporary entry** means entry into the territory of a Party by a business person of the other Party without the intent to establish permanent residence.

### ARTICLE 13.2: GENERAL PRINCIPLES

1.   Further to Article 1.2, this Chapter reflects the preferential trading relationship between the Parties, the Parties' mutual desire to facilitate temporary entry on a comparable basis and to establish transparent criteria and procedures for temporary entry, and the need to ensure border security and to protect the domestic labour force and permanent employment in their respective territories.

2.   This Chapter shall not apply to measures regarding nationality or citizenship, residence on a permanent basis or employment on a permanent basis.

### ARTICLE 13.3: GENERAL OBLIGATIONS

1.   Each Party shall apply its measures relating to the provisions of this Chapter in accordance with Article 13.2 and, in particular, shall apply expeditiously those measures so as to avoid unduly impairing or delaying trade in goods or services or conduct of investment activities under this Agreement.

2.   The Parties shall endeavour to develop and adopt common definitions and interpretations for the implementation of this Chapter.

3.   Nothing in this Chapter shall prevent a Party from applying measures to regulate the entry of business persons into, or their temporary stay in, its territory, including those measures necessary to protect the integrity of its borders, and to ensure the orderly movement of business persons across its borders, provided that such measures are not applied in such a manner as to nullify or impair the commitments made by a Party. The mere requirement of a visa or other document

authorising employment shall not be regarded as nullifying or impairing the commitments made by a Party under this Agreement.

### ARTICLE 13.4: GRANT OF TEMPORARY ENTRY

1.   In accordance with this Chapter and subject to the provisions of Annex 13A and Appendix 13A.1, each Party shall grant temporary entry to business persons who are otherwise qualified for entry under applicable measures relating to public health, safety and national security.

2.   A Party may refuse to issue an immigration document authorising employment to a business person where the temporary entry of that person might affect adversely:

   (a)   the settlement of any labour dispute that is in progress at the place or intended place of employment; or
   (b)   the employment of any person who is involved in such dispute.

3.   When a Party refuses pursuant to paragraph 2 to issue an immigration document authorising employment, it shall:

   (a)   take measures to allow the business person to be informed in writing of the reasons for the refusal; and
   (b)   promptly notify the other Party in writing of the reasons for the refusal.

4.   Each Party may set any fees for processing applications for temporary entry of business persons in a manner that is consistent with its obligations which are set out in this Chapter.

### ARTICLE 13.5: PROVISION OF INFORMATION

Further to Article 19.2, each Party shall:

   (a)   provide to the other Party such materials as will enable the other Party to become acquainted with its own measures relating to this Chapter; and
   (b)   no later than six (6) months after the date of entry into force of this Agreement, publish or otherwise make available in its own territory, and in the territory of the other Party, explanatory material regarding the requirements for temporary entry under this Chapter in such a manner as will enable business persons of the other Party to become acquainted with them.

ARTICLE **13.6:** DISPUTE SETTLEMENT

1.  A Party may not initiate proceedings under Article 20.6 regarding a refusal to grant temporary entry under this Chapter or a particular case arising under Article 13.2 unless:

(a)  the matter involves a pattern of practice; and
(b)  the business person has exhausted the available administrative remedies regarding the particular matter.

2.  The remedies referred to in paragraph 1(b) shall be deemed to be exhausted if a final determination in the matter has not been issued by the competent authority within six (6) months of the institution of an administrative proceeding, and the failure to issue a determination is not attributable to delay caused by the business person.

ARTICLE **13.7:** RELATION TO OTHER CHAPTERS

Except for this Chapter, Chapters 1 (General Provisions), 2 (General Definitions), 20 (Dispute Settlement) and 22 (Administration and Final Provisions), and Articles 19.2, 19.3 and 19.4, nothing in this Agreement shall impose any obligation on a Party regarding its immigration measures.

## CHAPTER 14
## ELECTRONIC COMMERCE

ARTICLE **14.1**: DEFINITIONS

For the purposes of this Chapter:

**digital products** means computer programmes, text, video, images, sound recordings and other product that are digitally encoded, regardless of whether they are fixed on a carrier medium or transmitted electronically[14-1];

**carrier medium** means any physical object capable of storing a digital product by any method now known or later developed, and from which a digital product can be perceived, reproduced, or communicated, directly or indirectly, and includes, but is not limited to, an optical medium, a floppy disk, or a magnetic tape;

**electronic transmission or transmitted electronically** means the transfer of digital products using any electromagnetic or photonic means; and

**using electronic** means employing computer and digital processing.

ARTICLE **14.2**: SCOPE

1.   The Parties recognise the economic growth and opportunity provided by electronic commerce the importance of avoiding unnecessary barriers to electronic commerce and the applicability of WTO rules to electronic commerce.

2.   This Chapter does not apply to measures affecting the electronic transmission of a series of text, video, images, sound recordings, and other products scheduled by a content provider for aural and/or visual reception, and for which the content consumer has no choice over the scheduling of the series.

ARTICLE **14.3**: ELECTRONIC SUPPLY OF SERVICES

For greater certainty, the Parties affirm that measures related to the supply of a service using electronic means fall within the scope of the obligations contained in the relevant provisions of Chapters 9 (Cross-Border Trade in

---

[14-1] For greater clarity, digital products do not include digitised representations of financial instruments.

Services), 10 (Investment) and 12 (Financial Services), and, subject to any exceptions applicable to such obligations and except where an obligation does not apply to any such measure pursuant to Articles 9.6 and 10.9.

### ARTICLE 14.4: DIGITAL PRODUCTS

1.    Each Party shall not apply customs duties or other duties, fees, or charges on or in connection with the importation or exportation of a digital product of the other Party by electronic transmission[14-2].

2.    Each Party shall determine the customs value of an imported carrier medium bearing a digital product in accordance with the Customs Valuation Agreement.

3.    A Party shall not accord less favourable treatment to a digital product than it accords to other like digital products:

  (a)  on the basis that:
    (i)  the digital product receiving less favourable treatment is created, produced, published, stored, transmitted, contracted for, commissioned, or first made available on commercial terms in the territory of the other Party; or
    (ii)  the author, performer, producer, developer, or distributor of such digital product is a person of the other Party,
    or
  (b)  so as otherwise to afford protection to the other like digital products that are created, produced, published, stored, transmitted, contracted for, commissioned, or first made available on commercial terms, in its territory.

4.    Paragraph 3 does not apply to any non-conforming measure described in Articles 9.6 and 10.9.

---

[14-2] Paragraph 1 does not preclude a Party from imposing internal taxes or other internal charges provided that these are imposed in a manner consistent with this Agreement.

## CHAPTER 15
## COMPETITION

**ARTICLE 15.1: PURPOSE AND DEFINITIONS**

1.   The purpose of this Chapter is to contribute to the fulfillment of the objectives of this Agreement through the promotion of fair competition and the curtailment of anti-competitive practices.

2.   For the purposes of this Chapter, anti-competitive practices means business conduct or transactions that adversely affect competition, such as:

(a)   anti-competitive horizontal arrangements between competitors;
(b)   misuse of market power;
(c)   anti-competitive vertical arrangements between businesses; and
(d)   anti-competitive mergers and acquisitions.

**ARTICLE 15.2: PROMOTION OF COMPETITION**

1.   Each Party shall promote competition by addressing anti-competitive practices in its territory, adopting and enforcing such means or measures as it deems appropriate and effective to counter such practices.

2.   Such means and measures may include the implementation of competition and regulatory arrangements.

**ARTICLE 15.3: APPLICATION OF COMPETITION LAWS**

1.   The Parties shall ensure that all businesses registered or incorporated under their respective domestic laws are subject to such generic or relevant sectoral competition laws as may be in force in their respective territories.

2.   Any measures taken by a Party to proscribe anti-competitive practices, and the enforcement actions taken pursuant to those measures, shall be consistent with the principles of transparency, timeliness, non-discrimination and procedural fairness.

**ARTICLE 15.4: COMPETITIVE NEUTRALITY**

1.   Each Party shall take reasonable measures to ensure that its government does not provide any competitive advantage to any government-owned businesses in their business activities simply because they are government-owned.

2.   This Article applies to the business activities of government-owned businesses and not to their non-business and non-commercial activities.

### ARTICLE 15.5: CONSULTATIONS

1.   At the request of a Party, the Parties shall enter into consultations regarding matters that may arise under this Chapter, including the elimination of particular anti-competitive practices that affect trade or investment between the Parties.

2.   During the consultations under this Article, each Party shall endeavour to provide relevant information to the other Party in order to facilitate the discussion regarding the relevant aspects of the matter which is the subject of consultations.

3.   Any information or documents exchanged between the Parties in relation to any mutual consultations under this Chapter shall be kept confidential.

### ARTICLE 15.6: CO-OPERATION

1.   The Parties recognise the importance of co-operation and co-ordination between their competition authorities for effective competition law enforcement in both Parties.

2.   Within six (6) months from the coming into effect of a generic competition law in Singapore, the Parties shall consult with a view to making a separate arrangement between their competition authorities regarding the scope and content of co-operation and co-ordination.

### ARTICLE 15.7: TRANSPARENCY

The Parties shall publish or otherwise make publicly available their laws addressing fair competition, including information on any exemptions provided under such laws.

### ARTICLE 15.8: DISPUTE RESOLUTION

1.   Nothing in this Chapter permits a Party to re-open, re-examine or to challenge under any dispute settlement procedure under this Agreement, any finding, determination or decision made by a competition authority of the other Party in enforcing the applicable competition laws and regulations.

2.   Neither Party shall have recourse to any dispute settlement procedures under this Agreement for any issue arising from or relating to this Chapter.

3.   In the event of any inconsistency or conflict between any provision in this Chapter and any provision contained in any other Chapter of this Agreement, the latter shall prevail to the extent of such inconsistency or conflict.

## CHAPTER 16
## GOVERNMENT PROCUREMENT

### ARTICLE 16.1: GENERAL

1.   The Parties reaffirm their rights and obligations under the WTO Agreement on Government Procurement ("GPA") and their interest in further expanding bilateral trading opportunities in each Party's government procurement market.

2.   The Parties recognise their shared interest in promoting international liberalisation of government procurement markets in the context of the rules-based international trading system. The Parties shall continue to co-operate in the review under paragraph 7 of Article XXIV of the GPA and on procurement matters in the APEC and other appropriate international fora.

3.   Nothing in this Chapter shall be construed to derogate from either Party's rights or obligations under the GPA.

4.   The Parties confirm their desire and determination to apply the APEC Non-Binding Principles on Government Procurement, as appropriate, to all their government procurement that is outside the scope of the GPA and this Chapter.

### ARTICLE 16.2: SCOPE AND COVERAGE

1.   This Chapter applies to any law, regulation, procedure or practice regarding any procurement by entities covered by this Chapter, as specified in Appendix 16A.1.

2.   For the purpose of this Chapter, a covered government procurement means a procurement:

   (a)  by an entity specified in a Party's Appendix 16A.1;
   (b)  by any contractual means, including through such methods as purchase or as lease, rental or hire purchase, with or without option to buy, of

goods or services or any combination of goods and services specified in
a Party's Appendix 16A.2; and

(c)  in which the contract has a value not less than the relevant thresholds
set out in Annex 16A.

3.  Except as otherwise specified in the Annexes, this Chapter does not cover
noncontractual agreements or any form of governmental assistance, including
co-operative agreements, grants, loans, equity infusions, guarantees, fiscal
incentives, and governmental provision of products and services to persons or
governmental authorities not specifically covered under the schedules to this
Chapter.

4.  In accordance with paragraph 3 of Article III of the GPA, the provisions of
this Chapter do not affect the rights and obligations provided for in Chapter 3
(National Treatment and Market Access for Goods), Chapter 9 (Cross-Border
Trade in Services), Chapter 10 (Investment), Chapter 11 (Telecommunications)
and Chapter 12 (Financial Services).

## ARTICLE 16.3: INCORPORATION OF GPA PROVISIONS

1.  The Parties shall apply the provisions of Articles II-IV, VI-XV, XVI:1,
XVIII, XIX:1-4, XX, XXIII, Agreement Notes and Appendices II-IV of the GPA
to all covered government procurement. To that end, these Articles, Notes and
Appendices of the GPA are incorporated into and made part of this Chapter,
*mutatis mutandis.*

2.  For the purposes of the incorporation of the GPA under paragraph 1, the
term:

(a)  **Agreement** in the GPA means "Chapter" except that **countries not Parties
to this Agreement** means **non-Parties** and **Party to the Agreement** in
GPA Article III:2(b) means **Party;**

(b)  **Appendix I** in the GPA means **Annex 16A;**

(c)  **Appendix II** in the GPA means **Annex 16B;**

(d)  **Annex 1** in the GPA means **Appendix 16A.1 of Schedule 1 of Annex
16A;**

(e)  **Annex 2** in the GPA means **Appendix 16A.1 of Schedule 2 of Annex
16A;**

(f)  **Annex 3** in the GPA means **Appendix 16A.1 of Schedule 3 of Annex
16A;**

(g)  **Annex 4** in the GPA means **Appendix 16A.1 of Schedule 2 of Annex
16A;**

(h) **Annex 5** in the GPA means **Appendix 16A.1 of Schedule 3 of Annex 16A**;

(i) **any other Party** in Article III:1(b) of the GPA means a **non-Party**;

(j) **"from other Parties"** in Article IV:1 of the GPA means **from the other Party**;

(k) **among suppliers of other Parties or** in Article VIII of the GPA shall not be incorporated; and

(l) **products** in the GPA means **goods**.

3.    Where entities specified in Annex 16A, in the context of procurement covered under this Chapter, require enterprises not included in Annex 16A to award contracts in accordance with particular requirements, Article III of the GPA shall apply *mutatis mutandis* to such requirements.

4.    If the GPA is amended or is superseded by another agreement, the Parties shall amend this Chapter, as appropriate, after consultations.

### ARTICLE 16.4: QUALIFICATION OF SUPPLIERS

Any conditions for participation in tendering procedures shall be limited to those which are essential to ensure the firm's capability to fulfill the contract in question. Any conditions for participation required from suppliers or service providers, including financial guarantees, technical qualifications and information necessary for establishing the financial, commercial and technical capacity of suppliers and service providers, as well as the verification of qualifications, shall be no less favourable to suppliers and service providers of the other Party than to domestic suppliers and service providers. The financial, commercial and technical capacity of a supplier or service provider shall be judged on the basis both of that supplier's or service provider's global business activity as well as of its activity in the territory of the procuring entity, taking due account of the legal relationship between the supply organisations.

### ARTICLE 16.5: INFORMATION TECHNOLOGY AND CO-OPERATION

1.    The Parties shall, to the extent possible, endeavour to use electronic means of communication to permit efficient dissemination of information on government procurement, particularly as regards tender opportunities offered by entities, while respecting the principles of transparency and non-discrimination.

2.    When each Party publishes a notice inviting interested suppliers to submit tenders for the contract in accordance with Article IX of the GPA, which is incorporated into this Chapter by paragraph 1 of Article 16.3, it will use a single point of access specified in Annex 16B.

3.   The Parties shall endeavour to provide each other with technical co-operation and assistance through the exchange of information on the development of their respective government electronic procurement systems.

4.   Pursuant to Article IX:8 of the GPA, the procuring entity shall publish a summary notice in one of the official languages of the WTO, namely English, French and Spanish. For the purposes of this Chapter, the Parties shall endeavour to use English as the language for publishing the notice for each case of intended procurement. The notice shall contain at least the following information:

(a)   the subject matter of the contract;
(b)   the time limits set for the submission of tenders or an application to be invited to tender; and
(c)   the addresses and contacts from which documents relating to the contracts may be requested.

### ARTICLE 16.6: PUBLICATION OF INDICATIVE PROCUREMENT PLANS

Each Party shall encourage its entities to publish, as early as possible in the fiscal year, information regarding the entity's indicative procurement plans in the electronic-procurement portal.

### ARTICLE 16.7: MODIFICATIONS TO COVERAGE

1.   Where a Party proposes to make minor amendments, rectifications or other modifications of a purely formal or minor nature to its Appendices to Annex 16A, it shall notify the other Party. Such amendments, rectifications or modifications shall become effective thirty (30) days from the date of notification. The other Party shall not be entitled to compensatory adjustments.

2.   Where a Party proposes to make a modification to its Appendices to Annex 16A when the business or commercial operations or functions of any of its entities or part thereof is constituted or established as an enterprise with a legal entity separate and distinct from the government of a Party, regardless of whether or not the government holds any shares or interest in such a legal entity, it shall notify the other Party. The proposed removal of such entity or modification shall become effective thirty (30) days from the date of notification. The other Party shall not be entitled to compensatory adjustments.

3.   Where a Party proposes to make a modification for reasons other than those stated in paragraphs 1 and 2, it shall notify the other Party and provide appropriate compensatory adjustments in order to maintain a level of coverage comparable to

that existing prior to the modification. The proposed modification shall become effective thirty (30) days from the date of notification.

### ARTICLE 16.8: TRANSPARENCY

The Parties shall apply all procurement laws, regulations, procedures and practices consistently, fairly and equitably so that their government entities provide transparency to potential suppliers.

### ARTICLE 16.9 : CONTACT POINTS

1. Each Party shall designate a contact point to facilitate communications between the Parties on any matter covered by this Chapter.

2. For the purposes of this Chapter, all communications or notifications to or by a Party shall be made through its contact point.

3. For the purposes of this Article, the contact points of the Parties are:

   (a) for Korea, the Ministry of Finance and Economy, or its successor; and
   (b) for Singapore, the Ministry of Finance, or its successor.

## CHAPTER 17
## INTELLECTUAL PROPERTY RIGHTS

### ARTICLE 17.1: DEFINITION

For the purposes of this Chapter:

**intellectual property rights** refer to copyright and related rights, trademarks, geographical indications, industrial designs, patents, layout-designs (topographies) of integrated circuits and rights in undisclosed information;

**TRIPS Agreement** means the WTO Agreement on Trade-Related Aspects of Intellectual Property Rights;

**PCT** means the Patent Cooperation Treaty administered by the World Intellectual Property Organization;

**ISA** and **IPEA** means the International Searching Authority and the International Preliminary Examining Authority, respectively, under the PCT;

**IPOS** means the Intellectual Property Office of Singapore; and

**KIPO** means the Korean Intellectual Property Office.

### ARTICLE 17.2: GENERAL OBLIGATIONS

Each Party re-affirms its obligations under the TRIPS Agreement, and, in accordance with the TRIPS Agreement, shall provide adequate and effective protection of intellectual property rights to the nationals of the other Party in its territory.

### ARTICLE 17.3: ENFORCEMENT

The Parties shall, consistent with the TRIPS Agreement, provide for the enforcement of intellectual property rights in their respective laws.

### ARTICLE 17.4: MORE EXTENSIVE PROTECTION

Each Party may implement in its domestic laws more extensive protection of intellectual property rights than is required under this Agreement, provided that such protection is not inconsistent with this Agreement and the TRIPS Agreement.

### ARTICLE 17.5: CO-OPERATION IN THE FIELD OF INTELLECTUAL PROPERTY

1.   The Parties, recognising the growing importance of intellectual property rights as a factor of social, economic and cultural development, shall enhance their co-operation in the field of intellectual property.

2.   The Parties, pursuant to paragraph 1, may co-operate in the following areas:

   (a) international search and international preliminary examination under PCT and facilitation of international patenting process;
   (b) promotion of mutual understanding of the other Party's intellectual property policies, activities, and experiences thereof;
   (c) promotion of education and awareness of intellectual property;
   (d) patent technology, licensing, and market intelligence; and
   (e) plant variety protection including exchange of technical expertise and knowledge.

### ARTICLE 17.6: DESIGNATION OF KIPO AS AN ISA AND IPEA UNDER PCT

1.   Singapore shall designate KIPO as an ISA and IPEA under the PCT for international applications received by IPOS insofar as these applications are submitted in the English language.

2.   Within three (3) months from the date of the signature of this Agreement, KIPO and IPOS shall conclude a Working Agreement for the detailed procedures in relation to the designation of KIPO as an ISA and IPEA as mentioned in paragraph 1.

### ARTICLE 17.7: FACILITATION OF PATENTING PROCESS

Singapore shall designate KIPO as a prescribed patent office in accordance with the Patents Act (Cap. 221) of Singapore and the regulations made thereunder for the purpose of facilitating the patent process of a patent application filed in Singapore that corresponds to a patent application filed in Korea, where the applicant for that patent application filed in Singapore provides IPOS with the necessary information, documents and translation on that corresponding application filed in Korea, as required by the Patents Act and the regulations thereunder.

### ARTICLE 17.8: PROMOTION OF EDUCATION AND AWARENESS OF INTELLECTUAL PROPERTY

The Parties may jointly undertake education, workshops, and fairs in the field of intellectual property for the purposes of contributing to a better understanding of each other's intellectual property policies and experiences.

### ARTICLE 17.9: JOINT COMMITTEE ON INTELLECTUAL PROPERTY

1.   For the purpose of effective implementation of this Chapter, a Joint Committee on Intellectual Property ("the IP Joint Committee") shall be established. The functions of the IP Joint Committee may include:

   (a)   overseeing and reviewing the Parties' co-operation under this Chapter;
   (b)   providing advice with regard to the Parties' co-operation under this Chapter;
   (c)   considering and recommending new areas of co-operation on matters covered by this Chapter; and
   (d)   discussing other issues related to intellectual property.

2.   The IP Joint Committee shall be co-chaired by senior officials from both KIPO and IPOS. The composition of the IP Joint Committee shall be decided in consultation with the co-chairs, subject to mutual agreement between the Parties. The IP Joint Committee may meet at the same time as when the Parties meet for the review under Article 22.1.

## CHAPTER 18
## CO-OPERATION


ARTICLE **18.1**: NON-APPLICATION OF DISPUTE SETTLEMENT PROVISIONS

Chapter 20 (Dispute Settlement) shall not apply to any matter or dispute arising under this Chapter.


ARTICLE **18.2**: INFORMATION AND COMMUNICATIONS TECHNOLOGY

*Co-operation in the Field of Information and Communications Technology*

1.   The Parties, recognising the rapid development, led by the private sector, of Information and Communications Technology ("ICT") and of business practices concerning ICT-related services both in the domestic and the international contexts, shall co-operate to promote the development of ICT and ICT-related services with a view to obtaining the maximum benefit of the use of ICT for the Parties.

*Forms and Areas of Co-operation*

2.   The forms of co-operation pursuant to paragraph 1 may include the following:

   (a)  promoting dialogue on policy issues;
   (b)  promoting co-operation between the private sectors of the Parties;
   (c)  enhancing co-operation in international fora relating to ICT; and
   (d)  undertaking other appropriate co-operative activities.

3.   The areas of co-operation pursuant to paragraph 1 may include the following:

   (a)  inter-operability of Public Key Infrastructure ("PKI");
   (b)  development, processing, management, distribution and trade of digital contents;
   (c)  business opportunities in third markets; and
   (d)  cross-recognition of professional ICT certification.


ARTICLE **18.3**: ELECTRONIC COMMERCE

1.   The Parties shall encourage co-operation in research and training activities that would enhance the development of electronic commerce, including by sharing best practices on electronic commerce development.

2.   Each Party shall maintain domestic legislation for electronic authentication that permits Parties to an electronic transaction to:

(a)  determine the appropriate authentication technologies and implementation models for their electronic transaction, without limiting the recognition of technologies and implementation models; and

(b)  have the opportunity to prove in court that their electronic transaction complies with any legal requirement.

3.   The Parties shall work towards mutual recognition of digital certificates through a cross-recognition framework at government level based on internationally accepted standards.

4.   The Parties shall encourage the inter-operability of digital certificates in the business sector.

### ARTICLE 18.4: SCIENCE & TECHNOLOGY

1.   The Parties, recognising the importance of science and technology in their respective economies, shall develop and promote co-operative activities in the field of science and technology.

2.   The Parties shall encourage, where appropriate, the co-operative activities between the private sectors of the Parties in the field of science and technology.

3.   The co-operation under this Article may include the following forms:

(a)  exchange of scientists, researchers, technicians and experts;

(b)  exchange of documentation and information of a scientific and technological nature;

(c)  joint organisation of seminars, symposia, conferences and other scientific and technological meetings;

(d)  implementation of joint research and development activities in fields of mutual interest as well as exchange of the results of such research and development activities;

(e)  co-operation in the commercialisation of the results of scientific and technological activities; and

(f)  any other form of scientific and technological co-operation agreed upon by the Parties.

4. The co-operation under this Article may include the following areas:

(a) biotechnology;
(b) nanotechnology;
(c) electronics;
(d) microelectronics;
(e) new materials;
(f) information technology;
(g) manufacturing technology;
(h) environmental technology; and
(i) science and technology ("S&T") policy and research and development ("R&D") systems.

## ARTICLE 18.5: FINANCIAL SERVICES

### *Regulatory Co-operation*

1. The Parties shall promote regulatory co-operation in the field of financial services, with a view to:

(a) implementing sound prudential policies, and enhancing effective supervision of financial institutions of either Party operating in the territory of the other Party;
(b) responding properly to issues relating to globalisation in financial services, including those provided by electronic means;
(c) maintaining an environment that does not stifle legitimate financial market innovations; and
(d) conducting oversight of global financial institutions to minimise systemic risks and to limit contagion effects in the event of crisis.

2. As a part of the regulatory co-operation set out in paragraph 1, the Parties shall, in accordance with their respective laws and regulations, co-operate in sharing information on their respective securities markets and securities derivatives markets, for the purpose of contributing to the effective enforcement of the securities laws of each Party. In this connection, the regulatory agencies of each Party shall be encouraged to formalise information sharing arrangement on securities markets and securities derivatives markets through a memorandum of understanding.

3. Articles 12.5, 12.8, 12.12 and 12.13 shall not apply to the co-operation between the Parties as set out in paragraph 2.

### *Capital Market Development*

4.   The Parties, recognising a growing need to enhance the competitiveness of their capital markets and to preserve and strengthen their stability in rapidly evolving global financial transactions, shall co-operate in facilitating the development of the capital markets of the Parties with a view to fostering sound and progressive capital markets and improving their depth and liquidity. The Parties shall, in accordance with their respective laws and regulations, give consideration to the implementation of linkage of exchanges located within the territories of the Parties, if both Parties determine that commercial interest exists for such linkage.

### ARTICLE 18.6: TRADE AND INVESTMENT PROMOTION

1.   The Parties shall co-operate in promoting trade and investment activities by private enterprises of the Parties, recognising that efforts of the Parties to facilitate exchange and collaboration between private enterprises of the Parties will act as a catalyst to promote trade and investment between the Parties and furthermore in Asia.

2.   The Parties recognise that certain co-operation between parties, one or both of whom are entities in their respective territories other than the governments of the Parties, could contribute to trade and investment promotion between the Parties. Such co-operation shall be specified in Section 1 of Annex 18A.

3.   The Parties shall review the co-operation set forth in paragraph 1 and, where appropriate, recommend ways or areas of further co-operation between the parties to such co-operation.

### ARTICLE 18.7: PAPERLESS TRADING

1.   The Parties shall co-operate with a view to realising and promoting paperless trading between the Parties, on the basis of the knowledge that paperless trading greatly contributes to the promotion of trade between the Parties.

2.   The Parties shall exchange views and information to study the development of paperless trading for a domestic electronic environment that enables the cross-border transaction between the Parties.

3.   The Parties shall encourage their relevant public and private entities to co-operate on the activities related to paperless trading. Such activities may include:

(a) the establishment and operation of facilities to provide paperless trading between the enterprises and their respective governments of the Parties;

(b) the joint studies on how to use and exchange electronic trade-related information and electronic documents and on possible action for standardisation and establishment of legal infrastructure; and

(c) the execution of the feasible pilot projects, including the electronic transmission of the trade-related documents, such as invoice, packing list and certification of origin.

### ARTICLE 18.8: BROADCASTING

1. The Parties, recognising the importance of broadcasting as a means for promoting cultural exchanges and understanding and the rapid development of broadcasting technology and innovative broadcasting services, will encourage co-operation in the field of broadcasting between the Parties.

2. The scope, form and other details relating to the co-operation in the field of broadcasting will be specified in Section 2 of Annex 18A.

### ARTICLE 18.9: ENVIRONMENT

Desiring to promote closer co-operation between interested organisations and industries of the Parties in the field of CNG technologies and applications to environmental protection, the Parties have concluded a Memorandum of Understanding to facilitate such co-operation.

### ARTICLE 18.10: HUMAN RESOURCES MANAGEMENT AND DEVELOPMENT

1. The Parties, recognising that sustainable economic growth and prosperity largely depend on people's knowledge and skills, shall develop co-operation between the Parties and encourage mutually beneficial co-operation between parties, one or both of whom are entities in their respective territories other than the governments of the Parties, in the field of human resource development. Such co-operation activities may include the following:

(a) exchange of government officials -

the Parties shall promote exchanges of their government officials with a view to enhancing mutual understanding of the policies of their respective governments and the details of such exchanges of such government officials shall be specified in Section 3 of Annex 18A;

(b) co-operation between educational institutions -

the Parties shall facilitate the launch of double degree programmes between higher educational institutions of the Parties, such as in the area of digital media technology;

(c) third country training programme -

the Parties re-affirm the importance of the Parties' Third Country Training Programme ("TCTP") in jointly rendering meaningful and productive technical assistance to third countries, in particular, in developing their social and economic resources and in recognition of the importance of the TCTP and its role in bringing the Parties' bilateral relations to a higher level, the Parties shall make effort to increase the current level of co-operation in the TCTP;

(d) ageing population -

the Parties shall exchange views and experiences on policy issues concerning an ageing population; and

(e) people developer -

the Parties shall promote the exchange of views and experiences on people developer between the Parties.

### Article 18.11: Maritime Transport

1.   The Parties, acknowledging the importance of maritime transport in their respective economies, shall develop and promote co-operative activities in the field of maritime transport. Such co-operative activities may include the following:

(a) exchange of maritime simulation instructors/assessors and Certificate of Competency ("CoC") examiners through study visits to learn how each Party uses simulators for their respective CoC training and other maritime applications; and

(b) development of a low-cost Automatic Identification System for marine applications such as fleet management for non-SOLAS vessels, monitoring of aids to navigation and monitoring of dumping activities at sea.

2. The Parties shall conduct consultation on specifying the co-operative activities and additional maritime co-operation in accordance with the Agreement on Maritime Transport between the Government of the Republic of Korea and the Government of the Republic of Singapore, signed on May 26, 1981.

### ARTICLE 18.12: ENERGY

1. The Parties, recognising the importance of energy in the respective economies, shall develop and promote co-operative activities in the field of energy.

2. The co-operation may include the following forms:

   (a) facilitation of co-operation between the private sectors of both Parties for the purpose of oil/gas exploration;
   (b) facilitation of co-operation between research institutes, and universities of both Parties for the purpose of engaging in joint R&D projects; and
   (c) exchange of information and sharing experiences in the fields of electricity and gas restructuring efforts, through study visits or such other activities as mutually agreed upon by the implementing authorities.

### ARTICLE 18.13: FILM PRODUCTION

1. The Parties, recognising the importance of the co-production of films in developing and expanding the film industries of both Parties and the potential for such co-productions to promote understanding and cultural exchanges between the Parties, shall promote co-operation in this area.

2. The scope, form and other details relating to the co-operation in the area of film production will be specified in the Section 4 of Annex 18A.

### ARTICLE 18.14: GAMING AND ANIMATION

The Parties, recognising both the potential of the gaming and animation industries as means for promoting understanding between the Parties and the rapid development of innovative media services, shall promote co-operation in this area between the Parties.

## CHAPTER 19
## TRANSPARENCY

### ARTICLE 19.1: DEFINITIONS

For the purposes of this Chapter:

**administrative ruling of general application** means an administrative ruling or interpretation that applies to all persons and fact situations that fall generally within its ambit and that establishes a norm of conduct but does not include:

(a) a determination or ruling made in an administrative or quasi-judicial proceeding that applies to a particular person, good or service of the other Party in a specific case; or

(b) a ruling that adjudicates with respect to a particular act or practice.

### ARTICLE 19.2: PUBLICATION

1.  Each Party shall ensure that its laws, regulations, procedures and administrative rulings of general application relating to any matter covered by this Agreement are promptly published or otherwise made available in such a manner as to enable interested persons and the other Party to become acquainted with them.

2.  To the extent possible, each Party shall in accordance with its domestic laws, regulations and procedures:

(a) publish in advance any such laws, regulations, procedures, and administrative rulings that it proposes to adopt; and

(b) provide interested persons and the other Party a reasonable opportunity to comment on such measures.

### ARTICLE 19.3: NOTIFICATION AND PROVISION OF INFORMATION

1.  To the maximum extent possible, each Party shall notify the other Party of any measure that, the Party considers, may materially affect the operation of this Agreement or otherwise substantially affect the other Party's interests under this Agreement.

2. Upon request of the other Party, a Party shall promptly provide information and respond to questions pertaining to any measure, whether or not the other Party has been previously notified of that measure.

3. Any notification, or information provided under this Article shall be without prejudice as to whether the measure is consistent with this Agreement.

4. Any notification, request, or information under this Article shall be provided to the other Party through the relevant contact points.

**ARTICLE 19.4: ADMINISTRATIVE PROCEEDINGS**

With a view to administering in a consistent, impartial and reasonable manner all measures referred to in Article 19.2, each Party shall ensure that in its administrative proceedings applying such measures to particular persons, goods or services of the other Party in specific cases that:

(a) wherever possible, persons of the other Party that are directly affected by a proceeding are provided with a reasonable notice, in accordance with domestic procedures, when a proceeding is initiated, including a description of the nature of the proceeding, a statement of the legal authority under which the proceeding is initiated and a general description of any issues in controversy;

(b) such persons are afforded with a reasonable opportunity to present facts and arguments in support of their positions prior to any final administrative action, when time, the nature of the proceeding and the public interest permit; and

(c) its procedures are in accordance with its domestic law.

**ARTICLE 19.5 : REVIEW AND APPEAL**

1. Each Party shall establish or maintain judicial, quasi-judicial, or administrative tribunals or procedures for the purpose of the prompt review and, where warranted, correction of final administrative actions regarding matters covered by this Agreement. Such tribunals shall be impartial and independent of the office or authority entrusted with administrative enforcement and shall not have any substantial interest in the outcome of the matter.

2. Each Party shall ensure that, in any such tribunals or procedures, the parties to the proceeding are provided with the right to:

(a) a reasonable opportunity to support or defend their respective positions; and

(b) a decision based on the evidence and submissions of record and, where required by domestic law, the record compiled by the administrative authority.

3.   Each Party shall ensure, subject to appeal or further review as provided in its domestic law, that such decisions shall be implemented by, and shall govern the practice of, the offices or authorities with respect to the administrative action at issue.

## CHAPTER 20
## DISPUTE SETTLEMENT

ARTICLE **20.1**: CO-OPERATION

The Parties shall at all times endeavour to agree on the interpretation and application of this Agreement, and shall make every attempt through co-operation and consultations to arrive at a mutually satisfactory resolution of any matter that might affect its operation.

ARTICLE **20.2**: SCOPE AND COVERAGE

1.   Unless otherwise agreed by the Parties elsewhere in this Agreement, the provisions of this Chapter shall apply with respect to the avoidance and settlement of all disputes between the Parties regarding the implementation, interpretation or application of this Agreement or wherever a Party considers that a measure of the other Party is inconsistent with the obligations of this Agreement or causes nullification or impairment of any benefit accruing to it directly or indirectly under Chapters 3 (National Treatment and Market Access for Goods), 4 (Rules of Origin), and 9 (Cross Border Trade on Services).

2.   Unless otherwise agreed by the Parties, the timeframes and procedural rules set out in this Chapter and its Annex[es] shall apply to all disputes governed by this Chapter.

3.   Findings, determinations and recommendations of an arbitral panel cannot add to or diminish the rights and obligations of the Parties under this Agreement.

4.   The provisions of this Chapter may be invoked in respect of measures affecting the observance of this Agreement taken by the relevant authorities within the territory of a Party. When an arbitral panel has ruled that a provision of this Agreement has not been observed, the responsible Party shall take such reasonable measures as may be available to it to ensure its observance within its territory.

5.   The Parties and the arbitral panel appointed under this Chapter shall interpret and apply the provisions of this Agreement in the light of the objectives of this Agreement and in accordance with customary rules of public international law.

### ARTICLE 20.3: CHOICE OF FORUM

1.   Disputes regarding any matter arising under both this Agreement and the WTO Agreement, any agreement negotiated thereunder, or any successor agreement, may be settled in the forum selected by the complaining Party.

2.   Once dispute settlement procedures have been initiated under Article 20.6 or dispute settlement proceedings have been initiated under the WTO Agreement, the forum selected shall be used to the exclusion of the other.

3.   For the purposes of this Article, dispute settlement proceedings under the WTO Agreement are deemed to be initiated upon a request for a panel by a Party.

### ARTICLE 20.4: CONSULTATIONS

1.   A Party may request in writing consultations with the other Party on any matter affecting the implementation, interpretation or application of this Agreement or whenever a party considers that any measure or any other matter that is inconsistent with the obligations of this Agreement or causes nullification or impairment of any benefit accruing to it directly or indirectly under Chapters 3 (National Treatment and Market Access for Goods), 4 (Rules of Origin), and 9 (Cross Border Trade in Services).

2.   If a request for consultation is made, the Party to which the request is made shall reply to the request within ten (10) days after the date of its receipt and shall enter into consultations within a period of no more than twenty (20) days after the date of receipt of the request, with a view to reaching a mutually satisfactory solution.

3.   The Parties shall make every effort to reach a mutually satisfactory resolution of any matter through consultations. To this end, the Parties shall:

   (a)   provide sufficient information to enable a full examination of how the measure might affect the operation of the Agreement; and
   (b)   treat as confidential any information exchanged in the consultations which the other Party has designated as confidential.

### ARTICLE 20.5: GOOD OFFICES, CONCILIATION OR MEDIATION

1.   The Parties may at any time agree to good offices, conciliation or mediation. They may begin at any time and be terminated by either Party at any time.

2.  Proceedings involving good offices, conciliation and mediation, and in particular positions taken by the Parties during these proceedings, shall be confidential, and without prejudice to the rights of either Party in any further proceedings under the provisions of this Chapter or any other proceedings before a forum selected by the Parties.

3.  If the Parties agree, procedures for good offices, conciliation or mediation may continue while the dispute proceeds for resolution before an arbitral panel established under Article 20.6.

### ARTICLE 20.6: REQUEST FOR AN ARBITRAL PANEL

1.  A Party may request in writing for the establishment of an arbitral panel if the matter has not been resolved pursuant to Article 20.4, within forty-five (45) days after the date of receipt of the request for consultations.

2.  A request for arbitration shall give the reason for the complaint including the identification of the measure at issue and an indication of the legal basis of the complaint.

3.  Upon delivery of the request, an arbitral panel shall be established.

4.  Unless otherwise agreed by the Parties, an arbitral panel shall be established and perform its functions in accordance with the provisions of this Chapter.

### ARTICLE 20.7: COMPOSITION OF ARBITRAL PANELS

1.  The arbitral panel referred to in Article 20.6 shall consist of three (3) members. Each Party shall appoint a member within thirty (30) days of the receipt of the request under Article 20.6. The Parties shall jointly appoint the third member who shall serve as the chair of the arbitral panel within thirty (30) days of the appointment of the second member.

2.  If the Parties are unable to agree on the chair of the arbitral panel within thirty (30) days after the date on which the second member has been appointed, they shall within the next ten (10) days exchange their respective list comprising four (4) nominees each who shall not be nationals of either Party. The chair shall then be appointed in the presence of both Parties by lot from the lists within forty (40) days from the date of appointment of the second member. If a Party fails to submit its list of four (4) nominees, the chair shall be appointed by lot from the list already submitted by the other Party.

3.   If a member of the arbitral panel appointed under this Article becomes unable to act, a successor shall be appointed in the same manner as prescribed for the appointment of the original member and the successor shall have all the powers and duties of the original member. In such a case, any time period applicable to the arbitral panel proceedings shall be suspended for a period beginning on the date when the original member becomes unable to act and ending on the date when the new member is appointed.

4.   Any person appointed as a member of the arbitral panel shall have expertise or experience in law, international trade, other matters covered by this Agreement or the resolution of disputes arising under international trade agreements. A member shall be chosen strictly on the bases of objectivity, reliability, sound judgment and independence and shall conduct himself or herself on the same bases throughout the course of the arbitration proceedings. If a Party believes that a member is in violation of the bases stated above, the Parties shall consult and if they agree, the member shall be removed and a new member shall be appointed in accordance with this Article. Additionally, the chair shall not have his or her usual place of residence in the territory of, nor be employed by, either Party.

### ARTICLE 20.8: TERMINATION OF PROCEEDINGS

The Parties may agree to terminate the proceedings before an arbitral panel at any time by jointly notifying the chair to this effect.

### ARTICLE 20.9 : PROCEEDINGS OF ARBITRAL PANELS

1.   Unless the Parties agree otherwise, the arbitral panel shall follow the model rules of procedure in the Annex 20A, which shall ensure:

(a)   that an arbitral panel shall meet in closed session;
(b)   a right to at least one hearing before the arbitral panel;
(c)   an opportunity for each Party to provide initial and rebuttal submissions;
(d)   that each Party's written submissions, written versions of its oral statement, and written response to a request or question from the arbitral panel may be made public after they are submitted, subject to clause (g);
(e)   that the arbitral panel may consider requests from non-governmental entities in the Parties' territories to provide written views regarding the dispute that may assist the arbitral panel in evaluating the submissions and arguments of the Parties;

(f) a reasonable opportunity for each Party to submit comments on the initial report presented pursuant to paragraph 3 of Article 20.11; and

(g) the protection of confidential information.

2. The arbitral panel may, after consulting the Parties, adopt additional rules of procedure not inconsistent with the model rules.

### ARTICLE 20.10: INFORMATION AND TECHNICAL ADVICE

1. Upon request of a Party, or on its own initiative, the arbitral panel may seek information and technical advice from any person or body that it deems appropriate. Any information and technical advice so obtained shall be made available to the Parties.

2. With respect to factual issues concerning a scientific or other technical matter raised by a Party, the arbitral panel may request advisory reports in writing from an expert or experts. The arbitral panel may, at the request of a Party or on its own initiative, select, in consultation with the Parties, scientific or technical experts who shall assist the arbitral panel throughout its proceedings, but who shall not have the right to vote in respect of any decision to be made by the arbitral panel.

### ARTICLE 20.11: INITIAL REPORT

1. Unless the Parties otherwise agree, the arbitral panel shall base its report on the relevant provisions of this Agreement, on the submissions and arguments of the Parties, and on any information before it, pursuant to Article 20.10.

2. Unless the Parties otherwise agree, the arbitral panel shall, within ninety (90) days after the last member is selected, present to the Parties an initial report containing:

(a) findings of law and/or fact together with reasons;

(b) its determination as to the implementation, interpretation or application of this Agreement or whether the measure at issue is inconsistent with the obligations of this Agreement or causes nullification or impairment of any benefit accruing to a Party under this Agreement, or any other determination requested in the terms of reference; and

(c) its recommendations, if any, on the means to resolve the dispute.

3. The Parties may submit written comments on the initial report within fourteen (14) days of its presentation.

4.   In case that such written comments by the Parties are received as provided for in paragraph 3, the arbitral panel, on its own initiative or at the request of a Party, may reconsider its report and make any further examination that it considers appropriate after considering such written comments.

### ARTICLE 20.12: FINAL REPORT

1.   The arbitral panel shall present a final report to the Parties, within thirty (30) days of presentation of the initial report, unless the Parties otherwise agree.

2.   The final report of the arbitral panel shall be made publicly available within fifteen (15) days of its delivery to the Parties.

### ARTICLE 20.13: IMPLEMENTATION OF FINAL REPORT

1.   The final report of an arbitral panel shall be binding on the Parties and shall not be subject to appeal.

2.   On receipt of the final report of an arbitral panel, the Parties shall agree on:

   (a)   the means to resolve the dispute, which normally shall conform with the determinations or recommendations, if any, of the arbitral panel; and
   (b)   the reasonable period of time which is necessary in order to implement the means to resolve the dispute. If the Parties fail to agree on the reasonable period of time, a Party may request the original arbitral panel to determine the length of the reasonable period of time, in the light of the particular circumstances of the case. The determination of the arbitral panel shall be presented within fifteen (15) days from that request.

3.   If, in its final report, the arbitral panel determines that a Party has not conformed with its obligations under this Agreement or that a Party's measure has caused nullification or impairment, the means to resolve the dispute shall, whenever possible, be to eliminate the non-conformity or the nullification or impairment.

### ARTICLE 20.14: NON-IMPLEMENTATION – COMPENSATION AND SUSPENSION OF BENEFITS

1.   If the Parties

   (a)   are unable to agree on the means to resolve the dispute pursuant to paragraph 2(a) of Article 20.13 within thirty (30) days of issuance of the final report; or

(b) have agreed on the means to resolve the dispute pursuant to Article 20.13 and the Party complained against fails to implement the afore-said means within thirty (30) days following the expiration of the reasonable period of time determined in accordance with paragraph 2(b) of Article 20.13,

the Party complained against shall enter into negotiations with the complaining Party with a view to reaching a mutually satisfactory agreement on any necessary compensatory adjustment.

2. If no mutually satisfactory agreement on compensation has been reached within twenty (20) days after the Parties have entered into negotiations on compensatory adjustment, the complaining Party may at any time thereafter provide written notice to the Party complained against that it intends to suspend the application to that Party of benefits of equivalent effect. The notice shall specify the level of benefits that the complaining Party proposes to suspend. The complaining Party may begin suspending benefits thirty (30) days after the date when it provides notice to the Party complained against under this paragraph, or the date when the arbitral panel issues the report under paragraph 6, whichever is later.

3. Any suspension of benefits shall be restricted to benefits granted to the Party complained against under this Agreement.

4. In considering what benefits to suspend under paragraph 2:

(a) the complaining Party should first seek to suspend benefits in the same sector or sectors as that affected by the measure or other matter that the arbitral panel has found to be inconsistent with this Agreement or to have caused nullification or impairment; and

(b) the complaining Party may suspend benefits in other sectors if it considers that it is not practicable or effective to suspend benefits in the same sector.

5. The suspension of benefits shall be temporary and shall only be applied until such time as the measure found to be inconsistent with this Agreement, or to have caused nullification or impairment has been removed, or a mutually satisfactory solution is reached.

6. If the Party complained against considers that:

(a) the level of benefits that the complaining Party has proposed to be suspended is manifestly excessive; or

(b) it has eliminated the non-conformity, nullification or impairment that the arbitral panel has found,

it may request the original arbitral panel to determine the matter. The original arbitral panel shall present its determination to the Parties within thirty (30) days after it reconvenes.

7.   If the arbitral panel cannot be reconvened with its original members, the procedures for appointment for the arbitral panel set out in Article 20.7 shall be applied.

ARTICLE 20.15: OFFICIAL LANGUAGE

1.   All proceedings and all documents submitted to the arbitral panel shall be in the English language.

2.   When an original document submitted to the arbitral panel by a Party is not in the English language, that Party shall translate it into the English language and submit it with the original document at the same time.

ARTICLE 20.16: EXPENSES

1.   Unless the Parties otherwise agree, the costs of the arbitral panel and other expenses associated with the conduct of its proceedings shall be borne in equal parts by both Parties.

2.   Each Party shall bear its own expenses and legal costs in the arbitral proceedings.

## CHAPTER 21
## EXCEPTIONS

**ARTICLE 21.1: DEFINITIONS**

For the purposes of this Chapter:

**tax agreement** means a convention for the avoidance of double taxation or other international agreement or arrangement.

**ARTICLE 21.2: GENERAL EXCEPTIONS**

1.  Article XX of GATT is incorporated into and made part of this Agreement, for the purposes of:

    (a) Chapters 3 (National Treatment and Market Access for Goods), 4 (Rules of Origin), 5 (Customs Procedures), 6 (Trade Remedies), and 14 (Electronic Commerce), except to the extent that a provision of those Chapters applies to services or investment; and
    (b) Chapter 16 (Government Procurement), except to the extent that any of its provisions applies to services.

2.  Subparagraphs (a), (b) and (c) of Article XIV of GATS are incorporated into and made part of this Agreement, for the purposes of:

    (a) Chapters 3 (National Treatment and Market Access for Goods), 4 (Rules of Origin), 5 (Customs Procedures), 6 (Trade Remedies), and 14 (Electronic Commerce), to the extent that a provision of those chapters applies to services;
    (b) Chapter 9 (Cross Border Trade in Services);
    (c) Chapter 10 (Investment);
    (d) Chapters 11 (Telecommunication) and 12 (Financial Services); and
    (e) Chapter 16 (Government Procurement), to the extent that a provision applies to services.

**ARTICLE 21.3: NATIONAL SECURITY**

1.  Nothing in this Agreement shall be construed:

    (a) to require a Party to furnish any information, the disclosure of which it considers contrary to its essential security interests; or
    (b) to prevent a Party from taking any actions which it considers necessary for the protection of its essential security interests:

    (i)   relating to the traffic in arms, ammunition and implements of war and to such traffic in other goods and materials or relating to the supply of services as carried on, directly or in-directly, for the purpose of supplying or provisioning a military establishment;

    (ii)  taken in time of war or other emergency in international relations;

    (iii) relating to fissionable and fusionable materials or the materials from which they are derived; or

    (c)  to prevent a Party from taking any action in pursuance of its obligations under the United Nations Charter for the maintenance of international peace and security.

A Party shall inform the other Party to the fullest extent possible, of measures taken under paragraphs 1(b) and (c) and of their termination during the meeting to review the implementation of this Agreement under Article 22.1, if such measures were taken.

## ARTICLE 21.4: TAXATION

1.    Except as set out in this Article, nothing in this Agreement shall apply to taxation measures.

2.    Nothing in this Agreement shall affect the rights and obligations of either Party under any tax agreement to which both Parties are parties. In the event of any inconsistency between this Agreement and any such agreement, that agreement shall prevail to the extent of the inconsistency. In the case of a bilateral tax agreement between the Parties, the competent authorities under that agreement shall have sole responsibility for determining whether any inconsistency exists between this Agreement and that agreement.

3.    Notwithstanding paragraph 2, Article 3.3 and such other provisions of this Agreement as are necessary to give effect to that Article shall apply to taxation measures to the same extent as does Article III of GATT 1994.

4.    Articles 10.13 and 10.19 shall apply to taxation measures to the extent that such taxation measures constitute expropriation as provided for therein[21-1]. An

---

[21-1] With reference to Article 10.13 in assessing whether a taxation measure constitutes expropriation,the following considerations are relevant:

(i) the imposition of taxes does not generally constitute expropriation. The mere introduction of new taxation measures or the imposition of taxes in more than one jurisdiction in respect of an investment, does not in and of itself constitute expropriation;

investor that seeks to invoke Article 10.13 with respect to a taxation measure must first refer to the competent authorities described in paragraph 5, at the time that it gives notice under Article 10.19, the issue of whether that taxation measure involves an expropriation. If the competent authorities do not agree to consider the issue or, having agreed to consider it, fail to agree that the measure is not an expropriation within a period of six (6) months of such referral, the investor may submit its claim to arbitration under Article 10.19.

5. For the purposes of this Article, competent authorities means:

   (a) for Singapore, Director for Fiscal Policy, Ministry of Finance, or his successor or such other public officer as may be designated by Singapore; and
   (b) for Korea, Deputy Minister, Tax and Customs Office, Ministry of Finance and Economy or his successor.

---

(ii) taxation measures which are consistent with internationally recognised tax policies, principles and practices do not constitute expropriation. In particular, taxation measures aimed at preventing the avoidance or evasion of taxes should not, generally, be considered to be expropriatory; and

(iii) taxation measures which are applied on a non-discriminatory basis, as opposed to being targeted at investors of a particular nationality or specific individual taxpayers, are less likely to constitute expropriation. A taxation measure should not constitute expropriation if, when the investment is made, it was already in force, and information about the measure was made public or otherwise made publicly available.

## CHAPTER 22
## ADMINISTRATION AND FINAL PROVISIONS

### ARTICLE 22.1: REVIEW ON THE IMPLEMENTATION OF THE AGREEMENT

1.  In addition to the provisions for consultations elsewhere in this Agreement, Ministers in charge of trade negotiations of the Parties or their designated officials shall meet within a year of the date of entry into force of this Agreement and then annually or otherwise as appropriate to review the implementation of this Agreement.

2.  Pursuant to paragraph 1, the Parties may:

    (a) review the implementation and application of the provisions of this Agreement including the work of any committees and working groups established under this Agreement;

    (b) establish and delegate responsibilities to any ad hoc or standing committees, working groups or expert groups to:

        (i)   assign them with tasks on specific matters;

        (ii)  study and recommend to the Ministers in charge of trade negotiations of the Parties any appropriate measures to resolve any issues arising from the implementation or application of any part of this Agreement; or

        (iii) to consider, upon either Party's request, new issues not already dealt with by this Agreement;

    (c) modify the established rules of origin and such modification shall come into force in accordance with Article 22.4; and

    (d) consider any other matter that may affect the operation of this Agreement.

### ARTICLE 22.2: CONTACT POINTS

1.  Each Party shall designate a contact point to facilitate communications between the Parties on any matter covered by this Agreement.

2.  For the purposes of this Agreement, all communications or notifications to or by a Party shall be made through its contact point.

3. For the purposes of this Article, the contact points of the Parties are:

  (a) for Korea, the Free Trade Agreement Bureau of the Ministry of Foreign Affairs and Trade, or its successor; and

  (b) for Singapore, the Ministry of Trade and Industry, or its successor.

## ARTICLE 22.3: ANNEXES AND APPENDICES

The Annexes and Appendices to this Agreement shall constitute integral parts of this Agreement.

## ARTICLE 22.4: AMENDMENTS

1. The Parties may agree on any modification of or addition to this Agreement.

2. When so agreed, such a modification or addition under paragraph 1 shall enter into force and constitute an integral part of this Agreement after the Parties have exchanged written notification certifying that they have completed necessary internal legal procedures and on such date or dates as may be agreed between the Parties.

## ARTICLE 22.5: ENTRY INTO FORCE

This Agreement shall enter into force thirty (30) days after an exchange of written notifications, certifying the completion of the necessary legal procedures of each Party.

## ARTICLE 22.6: TERMINATION

Either Party may terminate this Agreement by written notification to the other Party, and such termination shall take effect six (6) months after the date of the notification.

**ARTICLE 22.7: AUTHENTIC TEXTS**

The Korean and English texts of this Agreement are equally authentic. In the event of divergence, the English text shall prevail.

IN WITNESS WHEREOF, the undersigned, being duly authorised by their respective Governments, have signed this Agreement.

DONE in                 , on               , in duplicate, in the Korean and English languages.

| FOR THE GOVERNMENT OF<br>THE REPUBLIC OF KOREA | FOR THE GOVERNMENT OF<br>THE REPUBLIC OF SINGAPORE |
|---|---|
| BAN KI-MOON<br>Minister of Foreign Affairs and Trade | LIM HNG KIANG<br>Minister for Trade and Industry |